# THE IRON INDUSTRY OF THE
# FOREST OF DEAN

# THE IRON INDUSTRY OF THE
# FOREST OF DEAN

JOHN MEREDITH

First published 2006
Reprinted 2011

The History Press Ltd
The Mill, Brimscombe Port
Stroud, Gloucestershire, GL5 2QG
www.thehistorypress.co.uk

British Library Cataloguing in Publication Data.
A catalogue record for this book is available from the British Library.

ISBN 978 0 7524 3596 1

Typesetting and origination by The History Press

# CONTENTS

# FOREWORD

John Meredith tells the story of ironworking from prehistoric times up to the twentieth century, with the emphasis on the *story* – for this is not just a collection of facts and dates but a lively account of an important aspect of the Forest and of its place in history. From the expanding iron industry of prehistoric times through the Roman and Norman invasions and occupations up to the innovations and revolutions of post-medieval and modern times – here is the story.

But this is not a study in isolation, for the author also tells the story of ironworking in the Forest in relation to its hinterland – the areas and towns outside the Forest where the iron furnaces relied on Forest of Dean ores. The Roman towns of Monmouth and Ariconium were industrial centres which consumed hundreds of tons of Forest ore and it was also the Forest which fed the extensive medieval iron works in Monmouth and Trelech. The latter town, which is now a quiet village, was probably the biggest thirteenth-century settlement in Wales – the medieval Merthyr – six centuries before iron from the South Wales valleys built the British Empire. The Roman and medieval furnaces left vast drifts of iron slag which were in turn to fuel the first blast furnaces in the Wye Valley – the cradle of the Industrial Revolution.

The importance of the Dean in the history of Britain is displayed in the pages of this book, for John Meredith's *The Iron Industry of the Forest of Dean* is a volume that the general reader will find stimulating but which will also, I am confident, find a place on the bookshelves of many an academic.

Stephen Clarke
Monmouth Archaeological Society

# PREFACE

Knowledge of ironworking was probably introduced into Britain quite early in the first millennium BC. From a lake at Lyn Fawr in South Wales, amid a number of seventh-century BC items thrown there as part of a ritual deposit, came an iron sickle made in a form directly copying local bronze types. It was generally agreed that the sickle had been made locally. Subsequently, R.F. Tylecote has listed 47 British sites offering evidence of pre-Roman ironworking and almost half fell into the late Iron Age.

It is known that the production of iron was established in Asia Minor sometime around 2000 BC. Early production of iron commodities may have been sporadic but demand increased substantially by the end of the second millennium, with a rising demand for weapons. Like other techniques the knowledge of iron production would have been spread largely through people travelling and trading. It had reached Greece by about 900 BC and from there it spread onwards to Gaul and Europe.

Items of cultural trade, such as bronze implements and weapons, found within the British Isles confirms a link with the adjacent Continent particularly in the second and early part of the first millennium BC. Later in the first millennium trade routes became more established and, from the second century BC, the Atlantic zone of trade between Gaul and south-west Britain flourished until the later first century BC. The home port of the Atlantic route was Hengistbury Head, on the Dorset coast, where the Britons would have had contact with the sailors and traders from the Continent. Small coastal boats would have brought items for export to Hengistbury Head and the zone of coverage probably extended some distance up the shores of the Severn.

Other technologies were introduced into Britain during the Iron Age such as the manufacture of glass beads and bracelets and the use of lathes

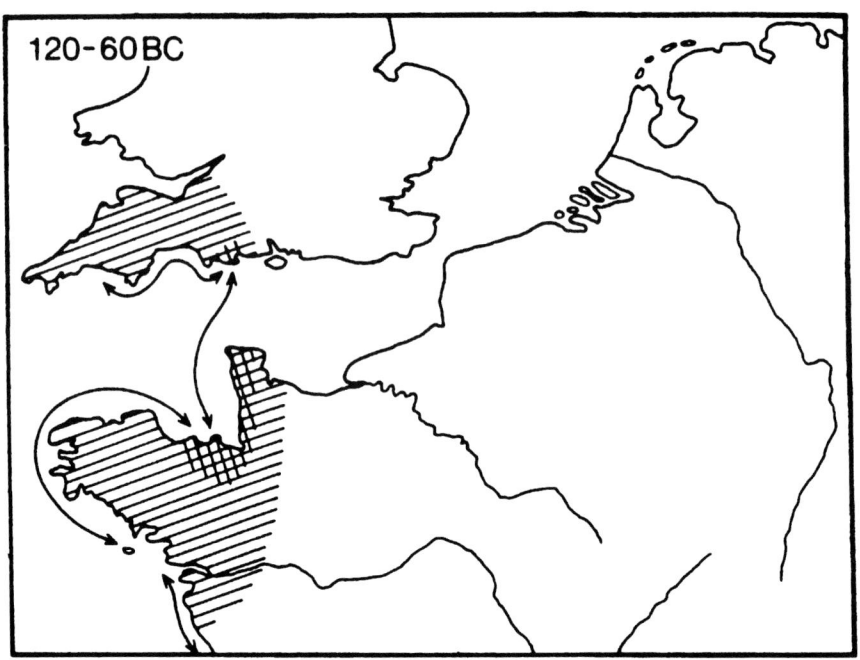

*1* Pre-Roman trade routes between Gaul and Britain. © *Barry Cunliffe and Daphne Nash*

to create vessels from shale. All this contributed to an intensification of production and, during the first century BC, there is evidence at Hengistbury Head of imports of Italian wine, raw glass and the contents of pottery containers made in Armorica, while potential exports included iron, non-ferrous metals from the Mendips and the fringes of Dartmoor and Kimmeridge shale. The Greek writer Strabo (64 BC – AD 21), writing at the end of the first century BC, confirmed the suitability of the sea crossing from Gaul to Britain when he wrote:

> The crossing to Britain from the rivers of Gaul is 320 stades [32 miles]. People setting sail on the ebb tide in the evening land on the island about the eighth hour on the following day.

Strabo is equally explicit about the range of goods traded. Exports from Britain included grain, cattle, gold, silver, iron, hides, slaves and hunting dogs. In exchange:

The natives were provided with ivory chains and necklaces, amber gems, glass vessels and other pretty wares of that sort.

The objective of this book is to explore the history of the iron industry of the Forest of Dean. It is soon evident that references are widely distributed, in various publications, with only a few attempts to provide objective accounts of some aspects of the subject. However, the story which threads its way through those references will provide a fuller picture of the Dean iron industry than previously given. This investigation commences by acknowledging the expertise of the British craftsmen prior to the arrival of the Romans.

Information from the preface taken from *Cross-Channel Trade Between Gaul and Britain in the Pre-Roman Iron Age.* © 1984 The Society of Antiquaries of London.

# ACKNOWLEDGEMENTS

In the preparation of this book I have received support from several sources and would like to thank the President of the Dean Archaeological Group, Dr Alf Webb, for his guidance and for allowing access to the Group's archives, our cartographer Geoff Gwatkin for the preparation of maps with his usual expertise, staff of the Public Libraries who were always willing to seek and produce the required books and my son, Owen, for producing the discs of text and illustrations.

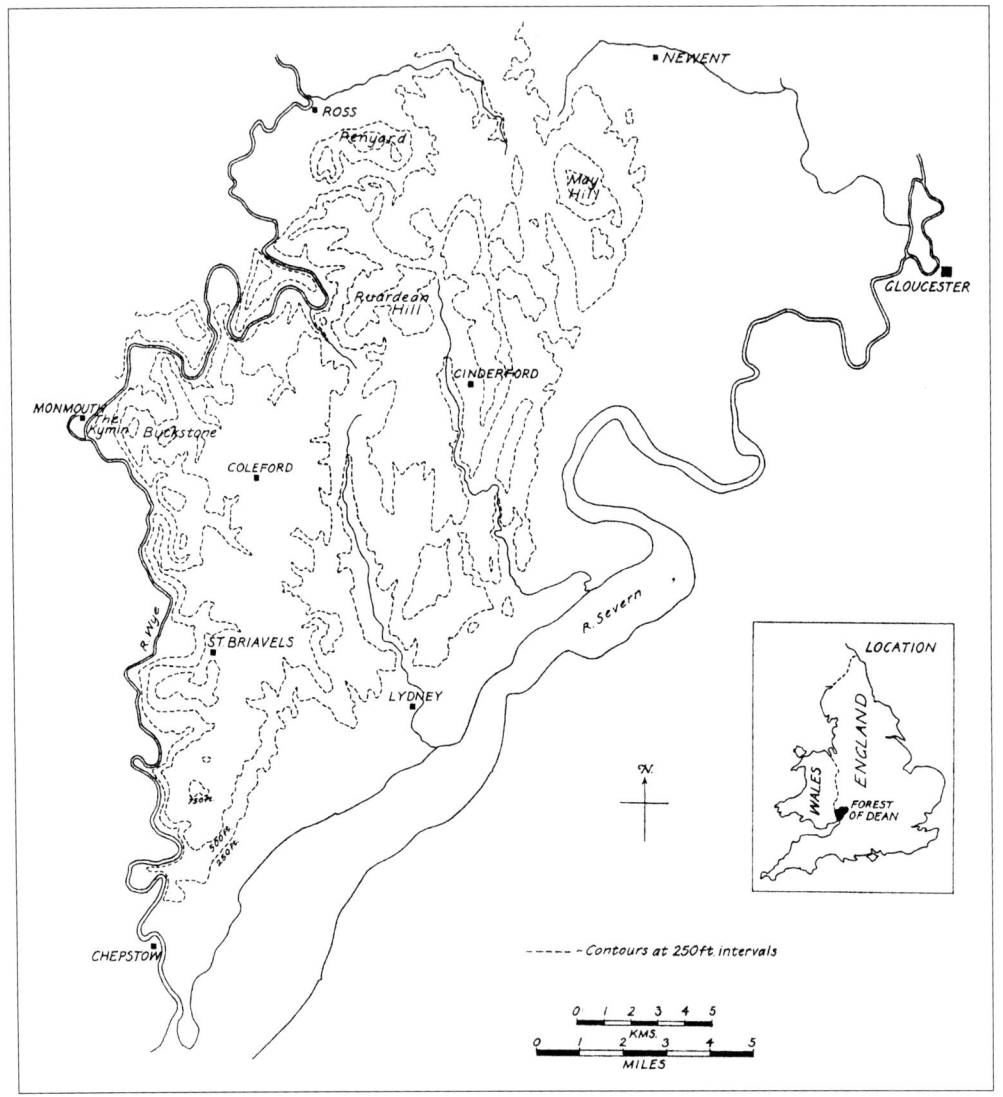

2 The Forest of Dean and its neighbourhood

# 1

# THE BEGINNING: THE BLOOMERY PROCESS

Since Domesday the area in which we will trace the history of iron production has been known as 'the Forest' and sometimes as Dene or Dean possibly after the Old English 'denu' or valley – perhaps the one to the east of Littledean where we find the remnant base of the Norman 'Castle of Dean' (Cyril Hart 1971). The region within which this lies is bounded on the western side by the River Wye, heading south to Beachley, and on the east and south by the River Severn also heading to Beachley where they join to feed the Bristol Channel. The northern boundary may be taken as a line from Ross-on-Wye to Gloucester.

There would have been extensive areas of natural wildwood covering the region in prehistoric times. Oak and hazel predominated but lime, ash and others prescribed a mosaic of timber excellence. When man progressed from hunter-gathering to the New Stone Age (Neolithic) he began clearing wooded areas for farming and by the mid-first millennium BC there would have been many small farming units in the region. People used timber for building, fencing and many other domestic applications but, despite inroads into the ancient wildwood, the Forest must have retained much of its original state because King Canute established it as a royal hunting forest in 1016 and this status was maintained by William the Conqueror. The Forest now covers approximately 30,000 acres (12,146ha) and is almost equally balanced between conifers and broadleaf trees, with oak accounting for about 36 per cent of the trees present.

An uneven plateau occupies the centre of the Dean area which has high sections to the north (Penyard, Ruardean and May Hill) and to the west

(St Briavels, Buckstone and the Kymin) but generally slopes gently towards the Severn. The area, of great scenic value, has some notable viewpoints and is dissected by two main valleys: one from the top of the Lydbrook Valley southwards through Cannop to Newerne and the other from Drybrook in a southerly direction through Ruspidge to Soudley.

The origin of iron can be traced back to the earliest igneous rocks on the face of the earth which contained many iron minerals, usually in the form of ferrous silicates. Natural weathering processes broke down the rocks and produced the final product of sand, clay and materials in solution. Desert conditions started about 270 million years ago and resulted in the 50-million year Permian period during which the Dean sandstones and shales of the coal measures were subjected to much deposition and erosion. Residual soils and rock waste built up on the land surface and in the subsequent rainy seasons iron solutions entered the underlying limestone, and the calcareous bands in parts of the Drybrook Sandstone, dissolving out the rock in the joints, and depositing pockets and veins of iron ore. Climatic conditions of rain and glaciations advanced the penetration of water through the joints, particularly in the Crease Limestone, where its box-like nature aided the formation of tunnels and caverns which formed the cave system. Some of the water picked up sulphur from the remains of the coal measures and created an acid, iron-bearing solution, which washed through the caverns and tunnels gradually encrusting them with iron ore.

There are several types of iron ore but the one found here is hematite, which is steel-grey to iron-black in appearance, and ranges from iridescent and dull to bright red when massive or earthy. The iridescent form of ore is goethite, generally found in a brittle stalactitic form but sometimes in botryoidal form, and is 40-62 per cent iron rich. The appearance of goethite led to it being known locally as 'brush ore' due to its resemblance to light brush woods. Red hematite is usually found in a relatively massive form, is very iron rich at 50-70 per cent, and is the deep red colour of the powdered ore. Ochre, known as 'colour' due to its use as a pigment in paints, is a native pigment composed of fine clay and an iron oxide and it is the origin of the latter which governs the colour which ranges through yellow, red, brown and purple. The ores often occur as dry powder and sometimes in a soft, semi-plastic form.

Red hematite was probably extracted as early as the Bronze Age (2000-500 BC) for some 'hammer stones', a spherical cobble and an oval-shaped spherical stone, were found near Drybrook in the Forest and they can be reasonably dated to the early Bronze Age. Spherical cobbles could well have been used to grind red ochre which was used from the early prehistoric period for 'dressing' bodies for burial, cave art and body paint and, from the Neolithic period, for decorating ceramics. A speculative interpretation of some stone tools found would put their period of use to the early Stone Age. The range of pigments produced were exported to Italy in the Renaissance during the fourteenth to sixteenth centuries. A small quantity of ore, for various purposes, is still produced at Clearwell Caves, near Coleford, and a quite extensive underground museum of the iron industry can be seen at this mine.

In the centre of the ar\ea is a geological basin where coal measures overlay the ancient rocks of sandstones and Carboniferous Limestone which contain amounts of the hematite iron ore, often exposed at the surface and readily accessible. The basin is roughly oval in shape with the greatest width of 8 miles (12.8km) from Cinderford to Staunton and the greatest length from Howle Hill in the north to Lydney Park in the south of some 12 miles (19km). The strata are steeply pitched on the east side of the basin resulting in ore penetration to 1000ft (300m) or more, while on the west side the strata is at a relatively shallow pitch where the ore penetrates to a general maximum of about 300ft (90m).

Hematite is very dense and has a specific gravity of 4.9-5.3, i.e. the ratio of the weight of a quantity of ore to the weight of the same volume of water. When subjected to a streak test, by being drawn across the surface of an unglazed porcelain tile, it usually gives a dark red to red-brown mark. Excavation in the early years was of the surface type when the rock was split by wedges driven by hammers. Lighter ore removal was by mattock or hammer and chisel and the latter tools are said to have left visible marks at some ironworkings at Lydney and Coleford. Sometimes quick lime was placed in crevices and water added which expanded the lime and split the rock. Fire was also used for the same purpose. The ore was gathered with scrapers and placed into baskets with oak shovels, roughly heart-shaped and approximately 9in (23cm) wide. The natural geological features of scowles, in the face of the exposed Carboniferous Limestone belt, often contain direct evidence of excavation, sometimes quite extensive, of seams of iron ore. Large pits and cavities were formed in the landscape where miners followed the irregular and winding courses of the iron ore, and sometimes these seams were followed further underground. Bog ores can also be found, off the limestone, formed by the action of weathering processes in

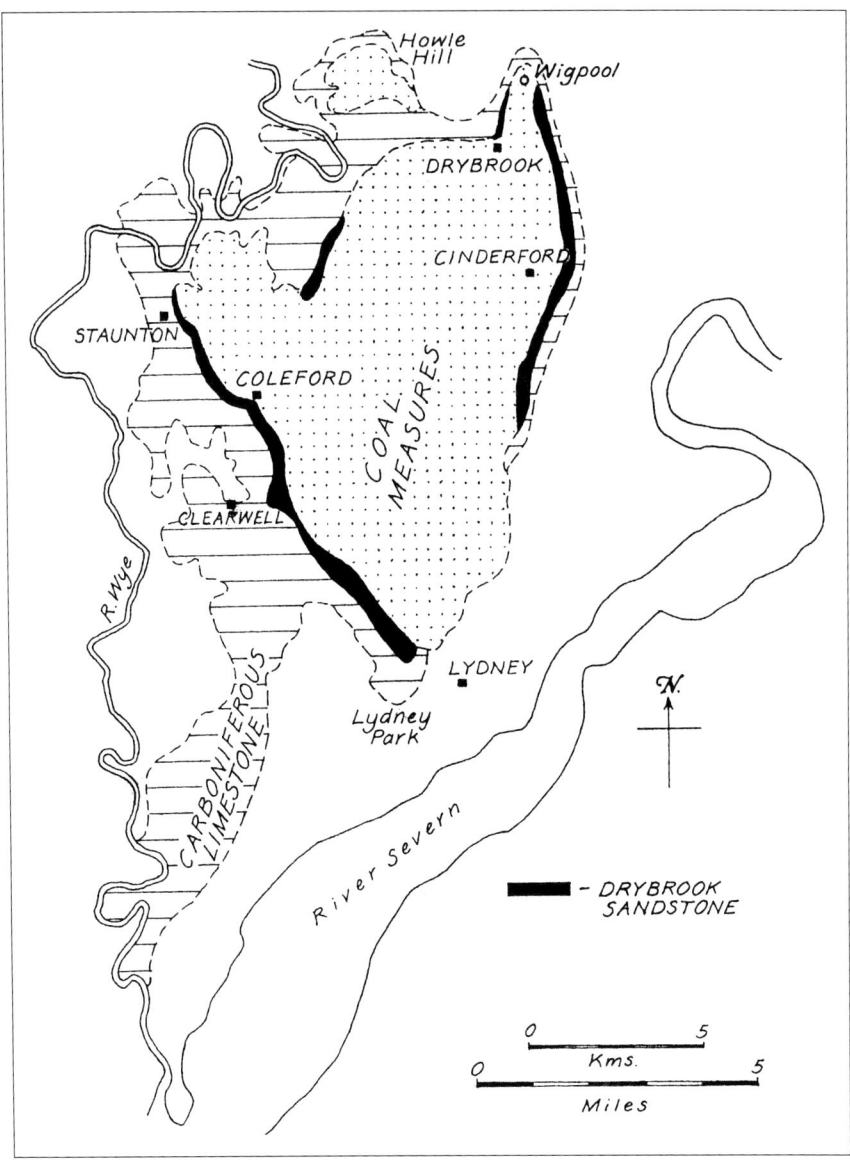

*3* Geological map of Dean showing the iron bearing areas of Carboniferous Limestone and the Drybrook Sandstone

acidic wet conditions on loose surface ore. Iron minerals predominate in this ore and they are known to farmers as iron pans.

Archaeologists have generally found only the base sections of any furnaces and occasionally portions of vitrified shafts or walls. Therefore we do not know exactly what an early furnace would have looked like. However, there are some better-preserved remains in Europe and in parts of the Third World iron bloomery smelting with small furnaces can still be seen today. Research and the reconstruction of furnaces, with which to experiment in the production of iron bloom, has provided us with a reasonably comprehensive view of early production processes and enough information to enable us to describe typical furnace operation in the production of iron from the ore. Excavation in some Iron Age hillforts has shown a pattern of post holes which might reasonably be assumed to indicate a shelter over iron-smelting activities.

The main principle in iron-smelting is the reduction of the metal oxide with carbon monoxide, which is formed by partial combustion of charcoal with the air induced to the furnace, and facilitates the reduction of the iron ore to iron. The effect of the carbon monoxide is improved if the ore is reduced in size to 1–2in (2.5–5cm) lumps as the reducing gas is then able to penetrate the ore more easily. There is a drawback in having all the ore reduced to quite small pieces because, although fine ore will be reduced rapidly, it also impedes the flow of gases in the furnace. Sometimes the ore is roasted in a fire which makes it more friable (easily broken) and also helps to drive out any moisture and impurities such as carbon dioxide and sulphur. Roasting also increases the porosity of the ore allowing the reducing gases to penetrate more easily.

Ironworking may be divided into two stages called smelting and hot forging. From early times bloomery smelting was the process used to produce iron at elevated temperatures and was employed during the Iron Age, the Roman period and up to around the seventeenth century at a local level. The melting point of iron is 1540 degrees Celsius, which could not be reached in these early furnaces. The ore contains unwanted minerals called 'gangue' consisting of silica, calcia and alumina which are slagged off at a temperature which can be achieved during the smelting process. The best ore for smelting is not necessarily that with the highest iron content but one with a high iron to gangue ratio because some iron is lost as a flux to the gangue in smelting, and more iron will be retained with a richer ore. Some elements such as manganese are of value in the smelting process because they replace iron as a flux in the slag, thereby increasing the yield of iron. However, it must be remembered that the yield of iron in the bloomery process was poor, as only 10-20 per cent of the iron in the ore was recovered.

Slags were run off in a liquid state at, or around, their melting temperature of 1250 degrees Celsius, i.e. below the melting point of iron. The iron, which was wrought iron, was produced as a relatively heavy sponge-like material which was called a bloom (hence the name of the process). This was generally removed from the furnace with tonges to be hammered, with several phases of reheating, to disperse adhering and entrapped slag impurities. In some cases the bloom was broken up and the small pieces of iron were separated by hammering; these pieces could be distinguished from the rest because they were ductile and would flatten upon hammering. These small pieces of iron were called hammerscale and they could be welded into a larger member by heating them in a smith's forge, followed by hot hammering. A rough block of partially compacted iron was produced which was nearing the stage of becoming a forgeable bar. Throughout this period charcoal was the fuel used in the production of good-quality wrought iron although there is some evidence for the occasional use of peat.

Although there were probably variations in the construction of furnaces, when we examine the basic methods of achieving successful smelting of iron from its ores two main types of equipment may be illustrated – namely a simple bowl furnace and a shaft furnace. The bowl was dug into the ground and lined with burnt clay possibly set on a heat-resistant stone lining placed on top of the earth. Bowl diameters ranged widely from 12in (30cm) to 60in (1.5m). A mixture of ore and charcoal was packed into the bowl and heaped above it. Experiments have revealed that it would have been necessary to cover the heap to allow the production of sufficient heat to achieve a reasonable yield of iron as an uncovered bowl would produce only a very small amount. Cover could have been made from turves but some form of bellows would have been necessary to build a heat level. Clearly the bowl method had some drawbacks as no slag could be run off and would therefore collect in the bottom of the bowl as a solidifying mass, often trapping quantities of unburnt charcoal and unreduced ore. The temperatures may well have been sufficient to produce a bloom above the slag cake and this could be removed for smithing, but the cake would have been prised out and discarded. Some bowl furnaces are said to have been

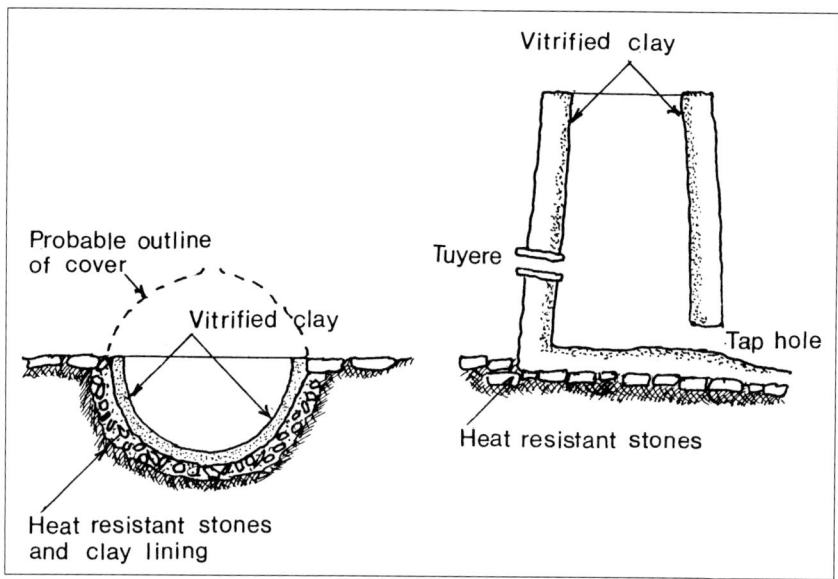

4 Section through a bowl furnace and a shaft furnace

covered with a clay dome with gases being vented through a hole in the top of the crown, but this would seem to preclude the periodic addition of charcoal and ore to the fire as it burned down.

There are two basic types of shaft furnace construction and the differences between the two concerns the superstructure, which is a clay tube with a bottom diameter of about 12in (30cm). In each case the base was constructed of a bed of flat, heat-resistant stones covered with a clay layer which would have reduced the absorption of ground water into the structure. In the first case, a tube of woven willow or hazel sticks formed a skeleton for clay cladding and in the other a tube was built up like a pot and 'grogged' with small pieces of heat-resistant stone. It is possible that the skeleton may have assisted the shaft construction but thereafter the rest of the furnace was constructed in the same way. At the base the walls would have been about 6in (15cm) thick with the sides sometimes tapering slightly towards the top, where they would have been some 4in (10cm) thick. The height of the furnace has been said to relate to the length of a human arm, based upon the reasonable assumption that access to the bottom of the furnace might have been necessary. On this basis it would have been about 18in (45cm) to 24in (60 cm) high. A hole, called a tuyere, was cut in the side to accommodate a bellows nozzle and another one cut at the base with a slope out towards the sand bed for the molten slag to flow out from. It is reasonable to suggest that, in order to achieve smelting temperatures and maintain them, a second tuyere would be required in the opposite side of the shaft.

Careful tempering of the inner face of the clay shaft was necessary to avoid damage due to initial thermal shock and, in experiments, wood fuel was used for this task because this partially vitrified the clay face and hardened the clay shaft. The slag hole and the tuyeres would act as flues for the firing which was done in stages ranging in duration from one hour to six hours or so, letting the furnace cool between firings and eventually producing a hardened furnace body. Generally the main firing mixture for producing bloom was found to be constituted of four parts of charcoal to one part of ore. Both the slag hole and the area around the bellow nozzles were sealed with clay. After obtaining a good heart to a charcoal fire at the base, layers of charcoal and ore were added until a charcoal layer brimmed over the furnace top. Layers would eventually burn through and regular top ups of charcoal and ore were needed. The temperature within the furnace could be judged from the colour of the flame which would progress from dull red to cherry red and then through yellow to white at which point smelting should occur. Removal of the clay blocking to the slag hole would allow the molten slag to flow out into the sand bed. The furnace would then be allowed to cool for two to three days. Sometimes slag would become deposited above and below the blow holes and would require rodding to release it. The sponge-like mass of relatively heavy bloom was sometimes attached to the side of the furnace and could be removed by chipping or with the tongs.

R.F. Tylecote (1986) has edited and illustrated proposals for several iron-smelting furnace types. All of these originate from modern research and ethnographic records and observations, particularly those from East Africa.

## FURNACE ONE

This is essentially a bowl furnace in which the charcoal and ore are separated – with the fuel receiving air, carbon monoxide, directly from the tuyere. The settlement of slag in the base is standard for this type.

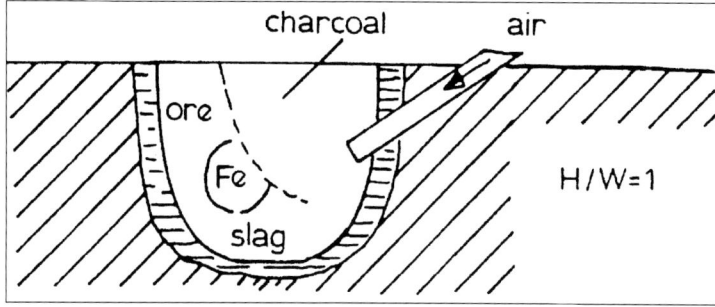

5(*a*) Shaft Furnace 1

## FURNACE TWO

The same furnace as the one described above with a type of chimney added and the charge mixed or layered. The reduction of the ore takes place in the upper part of the furnace but tends to get re-oxidised while passing the tuyere resulting in the metal tending to settle, with some charcoal and slag, at the bottom.

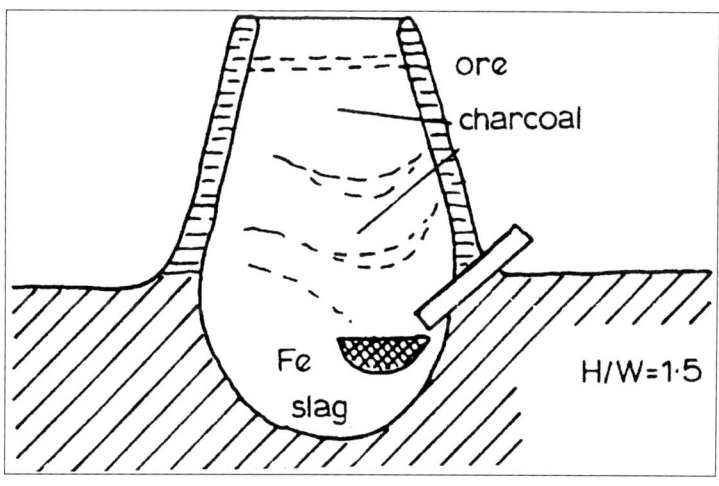

5(*b*) Shaft Furnace 2

## FURNACE THREE

This is an illustration of a furnace in which manipulation of the metal, by its removal at an appropriate time, from the region of the tuyere avoids re-oxidisation. It is essentially a bowl furnace of generous dimensions because the metal would have to be recovered from the top of the furnace. In considering a diameter of 39in (1.0m) more than one tuyere would be required and the furnace arrangement would have to be adapted to allow this.

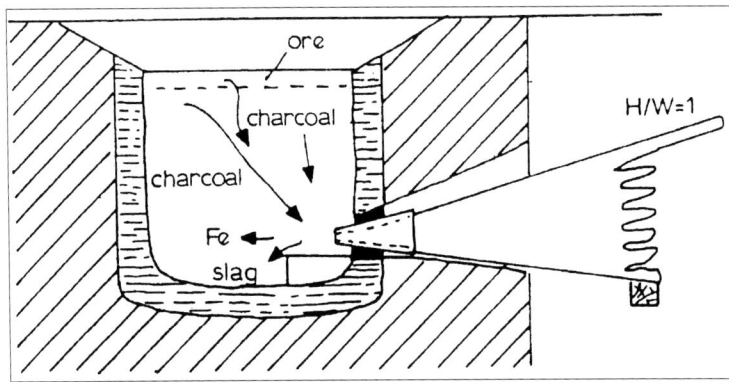

5(c) Shaft Furnace 3

## FURNACE FOUR

This is a development of the bowl furnace with a shaft that would help retain heat and the reducing atmosphere. This unit would require several tuyere and a slag pit for the collection of slag.

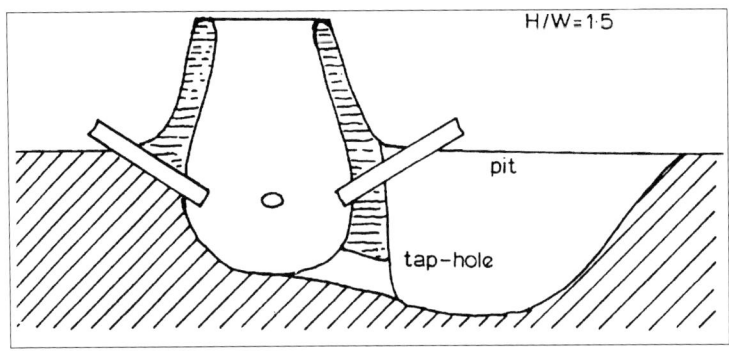

5(d) Shaft Furnace 4

## THE SHAFT FURNACE

Tylecote is of the opinion that the shaft furnace was developed from the bowl furnace shown as Furnace Two above and he also confirms the practical difficulty of differentiating between a bowl and shaft furnace when only the bottom parts remain. He confirms the necessity of keeping the tuyeres above the slag level as it is impossible to maintain an adequate pressure if physically blowing air into slag for an extended period of time. He illustrates two forms of shaft furnace, one banked and the other free-standing. It is perhaps permissible to comment on the apparent narrow width of the shaft, which would only be practicable if the bloom was always discharged at the foot of the furnace but not in the cases where it was recovered from the top.

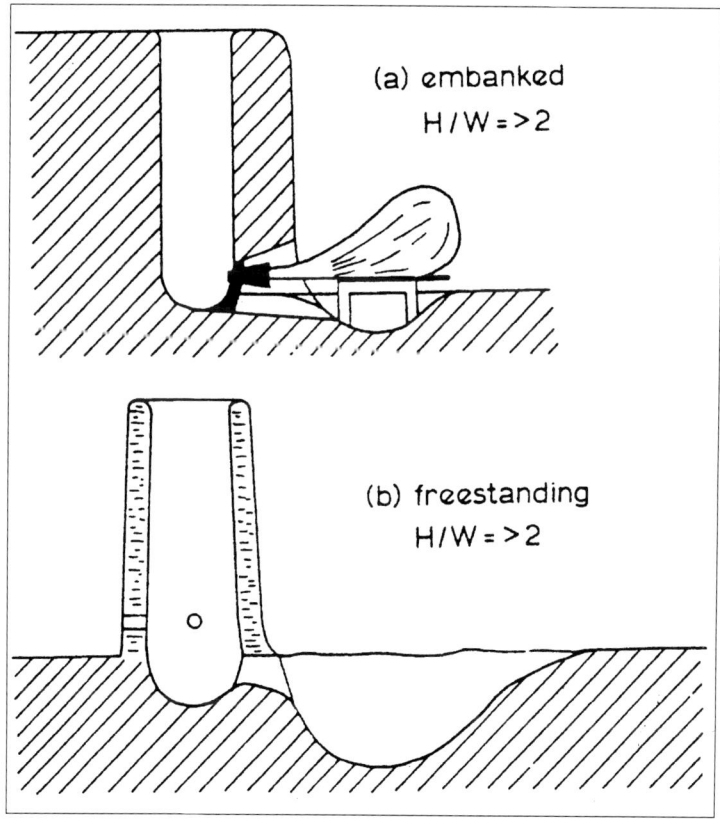

6 A shaft furnace, embanked and freestanding

## THE SLAG PIT FURNACE

One other type of furnace, called the slag pit furnace, has examples found in Northern Europe, the Sahara and in East Anglia. It is really a shaft furnace with a deep pit directly under the shaft into which the slag was encouraged to go at the end period of the smelt. After removal of the bloom the shaft was lifted side-ways to stand over a new slag pit. Experiments have shown that it was possible to move the furnace, if it was light enough, and examples proved to be reasonably strong. (Information taken from R.F. Tylecote, 1986.)

Charcoal burning is a very ancient industry utilised by man since his earliest attempts to extract metals from their ores and fashion them into utilitarian objects. Wood is composed of compounds of carbon and water and will burn at very low temperatures, so is not suitable for any use where high temperatures are required. However, when wood is treated to distillation in the absence of air the compounds are broken down and the gases driven off to leave carbon in the form of charcoal and a small quantity of ash. Charcoal burning was usually carried out by families, where a father and son would work together at the very skilled operation.

The following paragraph is the essence of an account of charcoal burning given to Brian Waters by Edward Roberts, one of the last members of a very long line of charcoal burners who started his own work at the end of the First World War (1914-18). Families like the Roberts' would have had a long tradition of being charcoal burners which likely stretched far back into history.

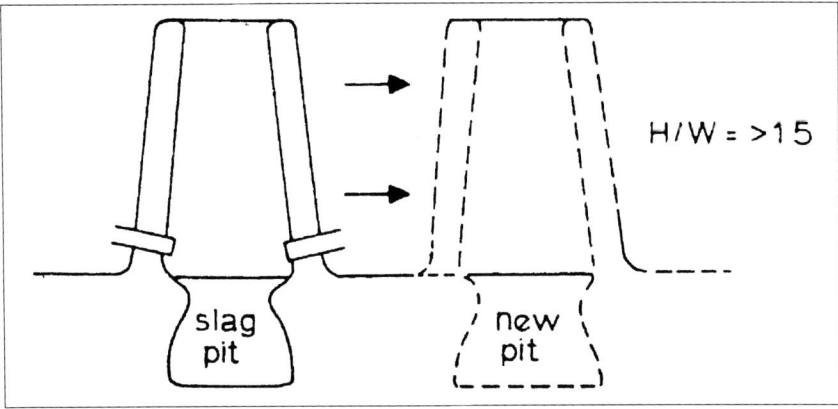

7 A slag pit furnace

A circle was set out with a diameter of around 16ft (4.9m) and a round pan dug out 18in deep (0.5m), generally into clay so as no draught was to come from below. The method of forming the central flue was to set up a tripod made of three lengths of cordwood. Lengths of cordwood were then built against the flue and, as the stack increased, they tended to work gradually to an inward slant. Sticks were added around the stack in turn until the stack was about 5ft (1.5m) high and some 8yds (7.3m) across. The construction was then covered with turf, the centre ignited at the bottom of the central flue, and a steel plate set to seal the top of the flue. Soon the smoke began to pour out of vent holes left open at around 3ft (1.0m) intervals at the base of the stack. The pit had to be attended every two hours and the very longest that it could be left was four hours. Sometimes the crust of turves would crack and show a blue flame like a gas jet. Burning was allowed to continue for four days and was finished when no more smoke was issuing from the vents. Twenty hours had to be left before the pit would be cool enough for the charcoal to be handled. The type of pit described would take as much as 10 tons (10.160 tonnes) of wood and yield 2.5 tons (2.535 tonnes) of charcoal. (Information taken from B. Waters *The Forest of Dean*.)

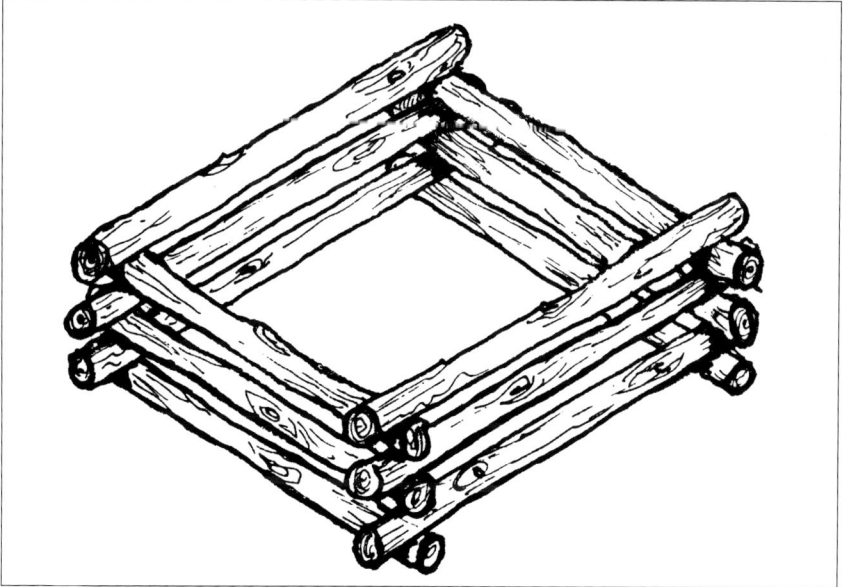

*8* One method of forming a flue in a charcoal stack

The following is a recent account of a charcoal-burning display at the Dean Heritage Centre at Soudley and contains details of the methods employed by other foresters.

A dome-shaped stack up to 6ft 6in (2m) high and some 20ft (6m) in diameter was built of small tree growth, coppiced growth or branches of hardwood around a central flue formed as shown in the accompanying diagram (*8*). No conifer was used in charcoal production. The stack was covered with sods and earth, with several flues left around the base. A fire was started in the flue at the heart of the stack and, once the wood near the core had been burnt, the inlet flues were gradually closed leaving the remaining wood with insufficient heat to burn but enough to drive off the compounds as gases. The central flue was then capped with a metal plate. As the process progressed some holes were carefully opened higher up the stack to allow the gradual egress of smoke and gases. The stack had to be watched almost constantly for fear of a collapse in the covering which would allow too much air to enter and result in the stack being destroyed by fire. The charcoal burners had an adjacent hut for shelter of the resting party and the watcher sometimes had to sit on a one-legged stool which would throw him off if he dozed! Stopping the process was a delicate operation as a rush of air into a stack which was not cold would result in the whole structure catching fire. A change in the colour of smoke from white to blue indicated that the stage had been reached when the charcoal was complete, but several more days were allowed for the stack to cool while construction of the next stack was commenced. When the stack was opened water was often to hand to douse any 'lively' charcoal. The final operation was to sort through the charcoal and discard any partly burned ends of timber from the stack.

Evidence of earlier charcoal burning is still evident today when some fields are ploughed, with the characteristic grey-black rings from charcoal stacks being easily recognisable. Five tonnes of timber yielded one tonne of charcoal. In 1282 records show that 2292 charcoal hearths were still visible in Dean, some in use, some abandoned (B. Walters 1992).

There are some aspects of the results of relatively recent archaeological investigation which it will be useful to consider here, starting with the rates of production. Experimental work has led to the assumption that the smelting of 1 tonne of ore in a shaft furnace would require 1 tonne of charcoal which would produce 1200lb (540kg) of slag and 728lb (330kg) of bloom. Primary smithing of that bloom would produce some 330lb (150kg)

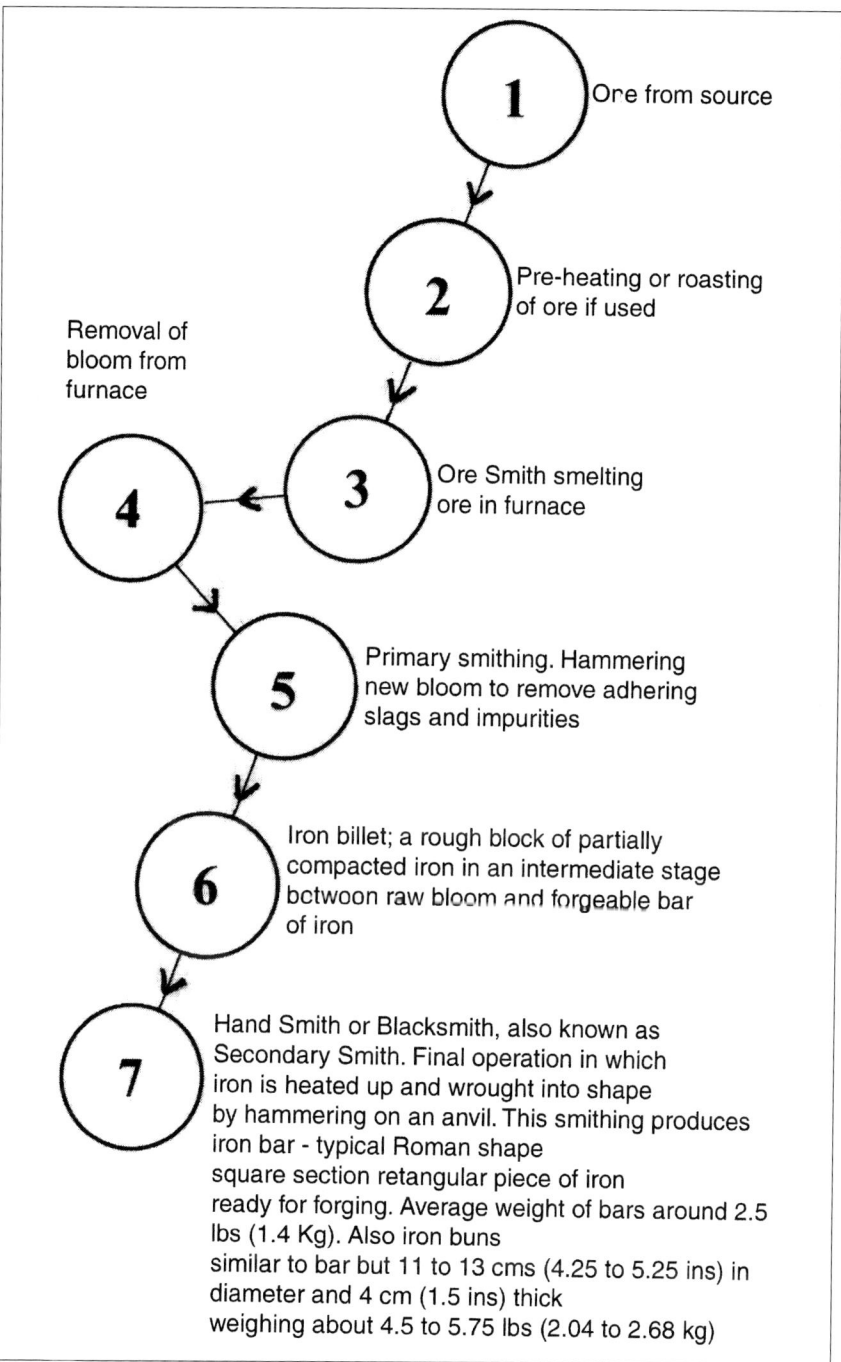

1 Ore from source

2 Pre-heating or roasting of ore if used

Removal of bloom from furnace

4

3 Ore Smith smelting ore in furnace

5 Primary smithing. Hammering new bloom to remove adhering slags and impurities

6 Iron billet; a rough block of partially compacted iron in an intermediate stage betwoon raw bloom and forgeable bar of iron

7 Hand Smith or Blacksmith, also known as Secondary Smith. Final operation in which iron is heated up and wrought into shape by hammering on an anvil. This smithing produces iron bar - typical Roman shape square section retangular piece of iron ready for forging. Average weight of bars around 2.5 lbs (1.4 Kg). Also iron buns similar to bar but 11 to 13 cms (4.25 to 5.25 ins) in diameter and 4 cm (1.5 ins) thick weighing about 4.5 to 5.75 lbs (2.04 to 2.68 kg)

9 Iron working in the bloomery period from ore to blacksmith

of billet resulting in 165lb (75kg) of iron ready for forging. Turning to the requirement for charcoal fuel, it has been estimated that about 2.5 acres (1ha) of coppiced woodland would produce about 1 tonne of charcoal per year, and that means that one smelting furnace would require about 22.5 acres (9ha) of coppiced wood per annum. This requirement is for smelting only so any time gap between that and smithing, resulting in cooling of the material, would therefore require several times as much charcoal to complete the process. It is interesting to note that the bulk of slag produced at the commencement of the above process is over seven times the weight of the resulting iron ready for forging. This goes some way to explaining the immense quantities of slag which will be noted at all sites in the following pages and the fact that between 50-80 per cent of the iron in the ore will have been lost to the slag in the smelting.

The wide area of iron production around Dean has frequently raised the question regarding the origin of the ore. During the Roman period smelting is documented throughout Gloucestershire, south Worcestershire and Herefordshire and into Gwent. Analysis of ores from these areas has confirmed their origin as Dean, with a strong emphasis on eastern Dean sources including Wigpool which has always been considered as the principal source for Ariconium. There is a tradition in the Dean iron industry of smelting ores at some distance from their source. It may be that ores were taken to areas where charcoal fuel was being produced or that some aspect of distributing ores to different tribal groups in the area may have survived from the Iron Age.

# 2

# IRON AGE TO THE SECOND CENTURY AD

The surviving archaeological evidence of the period which preceded 700 BC seems to indicate conservation of systems, showing no signs of innovation or development of new ideas. However, the new specialist skill of bronze casting can be identified although this was probably in the hands of a relatively small number of individuals. During the eighth century trading contacts expanded and imported wares inspired local industry to develop and increase the distribution of cheaper bronzes. This phase of innovation inspired social, economic and technical changes which formed the basis for the beginning of the Iron Age.

The early Iron Age hilltop enclosures, while being communal structures, did not exhibit evidence of continuous occupation and it is likely that most people would have been established in surrounding farmsteads where various domestic crafts, including occasional iron-smelting, would have been carried out. The hilltop enclosures would have been used as places of celebration, feasting, trading and storage. Only later in the Iron Age did they become progressively more defended structures when the population increased, partially due to climate deterioration forcing people who farmed at higher altitudes on to land at lower levels. The hierarchy of each social unit would have felt it necessary to secure the lands which provided the food for their people, and the enclosure of farmlands would have been followed by more defensive provision at the hilltop enclosure.

Pottery was handmade by the ring-coil method and fired in bonfire kilns with various styles relating to the particular hilltop enclosure of origin. From the fifth and the fourth centuries BC pottery styles began to change.

One product of interest was the All Cannings Cross pottery which later became the All Cannings Cross-Meon Hill (Hampshire) pottery, noted for its hematite coating on bowls which, when burnished, had the delightful appearance of bronze. From the fourth century BC onwards plain, coarse pottery called 'Iron Age B coarse ware,' occurred and typically existed in the form of plain jars, bowls and barrel jars. From the third to the first century BC the 'saucepan pot tradition' developed, decorated either with bands of stamped impressions below the rim or with a similarly placed zone of linear tooling. This pottery was from the Croft Ambrey-Bredon Hill (Herefordshire–Worcestershire) source and was distributed to an area which had hitherto been largely aceramic. The Lydney-Llanmelin style of 'saucepan pot' was of a distinctive style with decoration including chevron patterns and large oval-shaped stab marks peculiar to this product. This pottery came from a group of sites in an area east of Usk and within a few miles of Dean. Although the potter's wheel was introduced into southern Britain in the period 150-50 BC it is likely that traditional methods of production in what is now Gloucestershire, Herefordshire, Shropshire and South Wales would have continued well into the first century AD.

While most areas of Britain lay within easy reach of iron ore deposits the methods of collection and smelting would have developed over time. We have mentioned the sickle from Llyn Fawr, Glamorgan, less than 40 miles west of the Forest of Dean, dated to the seventh century BC, which

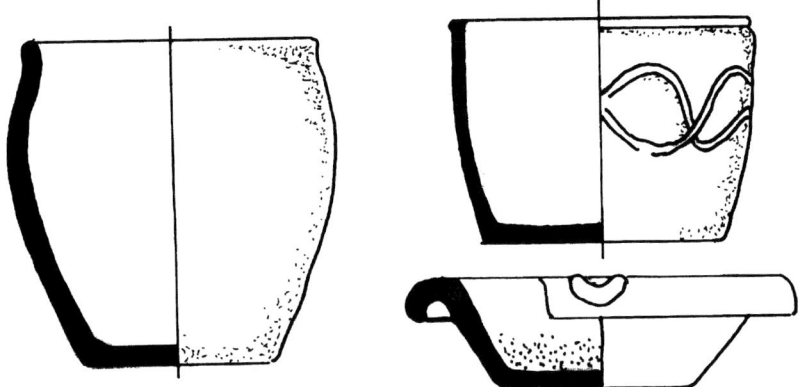

*10 Above:* This is 'Iron Age B coarse ware', about 6in (15cm) bottom diameter
*11 Above right:* Iron Age saucepan pot, about 5in (13cm) bottom diameter
*12 Right:* Iron Age mortarium with internal trituration, a 'mixing bowl', about 8in (20cm) bottom diameter

indicated that a competent blacksmith had crafted this item. Llyn Fawr also contained a spear and a sword. We know that sword-makers were generally itinerant craftsmen who moved between settlements and made, or repaired, swords for the occupants. In Essex a cauldron of the early seventh century BC was found, together with an iron stud, and a hoard from Sussex contained a mass of corroded iron of indistinguishable form.

The change over from bronze to iron in common use would have been very gradual and would have started with bronze items being copied in iron. Tradition lingered for centuries and late Bronze Age types were found in Iron Age sites and it was not until the third or fourth centuries BC that iron came into more common use. Smelting and forging seem to have been carried out at homestead level and two examples of this are interesting. At Kestor, Devon, a large hut, 37ft (11.3m) across, had a central roof opening with a rainwater drip-pit beneath and contained a small bowl furnace, some 12-18in (30-45cm) in diameter, and dug to a depth of 9in (23cm) below the floor. On one side lay a flat stone possibly used as a bellows rest. Charcoal and cinders with a high iron content were found within the furnace. Nearby was a larger pit, discoloured by intense heat, which was probably used to reheat the bloom for forging. In the early palisaded homestead of West Brandon, Co. Durham, two simple bowl furnaces were discovered, each about 12in (30cm) in diameter and 8in (21cm) deep. One of them had a groove, in which the tuyere would have been placed, and contained the broken-up remains of a clay dome, showing that it had been, at least partially, enclosed. While only a few furnaces have been found, wide deposits of slag and cinder indicate that the skill of extraction and forging was at a domestic level in the early years. (Information taken from B. Cunliffe, 1978.)

In 1986, R.F. Tylecote identified several early Iron Age sites in Gloucestershire and Gwent and, whilst there would have been more, his sites are worth recording: Bagendon, Glos., AD 10-50, Merthyr-Mawr Warren, Glam., fourth to first century BC, Mynydd Bychan, Glam., 150 BC to AD 100, and Sudbrook, Gwent, first century BC to first century AD. Sudbrook is a promontory fort located just 4 miles from the southernmost tip of the Forest of Dean on the Severn Estuary at a very ancient crossing point of the Severn. River action has eroded some of the fort but its position suggests that it was an important trading point and some of the Dean iron must surely have left here for export to Gaul. There is an inherent difficulty in identifying smelting sites within the tree cover of Dean for we know,

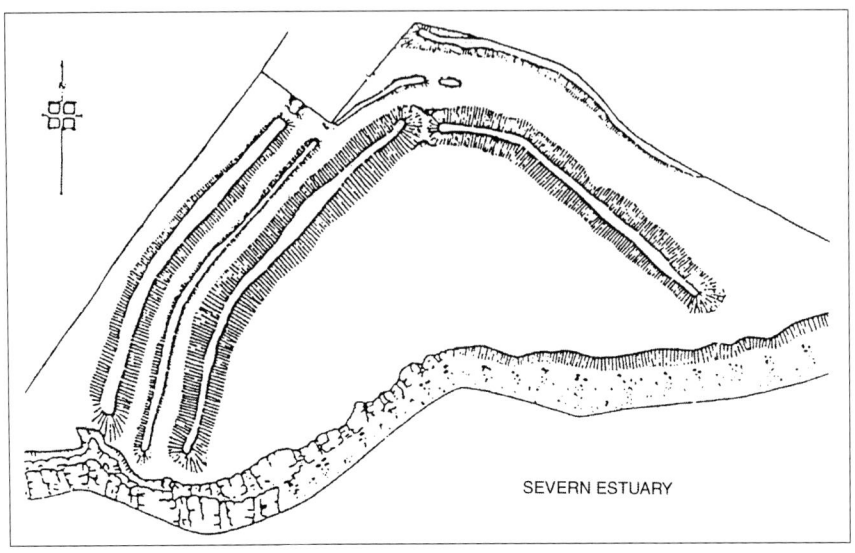

*13* Plan of Sudbrook Camp after Nash-Williams, 1936

from aerial photographs, that a site denuded of trees can be covered with woodland within several decades.

## CURRENCY BARS

The village of Glastonbury, in Somerset, was a village of some 3.5 acres (1.42ha), built on an artificial island in a lake. Over 60 floors of circular huts were discovered and smiths who worked in bronze and iron manufactured many tools, both industrial and domestic. Iron sickles, bill hooks, forged chisels, gouges, saws etc. were of a common pattern and found throughout Britain, and sometimes in Scotland and Ireland. The settlement existed from the second century BC until it was destroyed in the middle of the first century AD. A waterway to the Bristol Channel, which was only 12 miles (19.3km) distant, made waterborne traffic possible and local land routes were important for trade. The village really was a centre of trade and this was borne out by the discovery of currency bars on the site.

Currency bars were peculiarly-shaped objects of iron, mostly around 3ft (1.0m) long and resembling a half-finished sword, having a roughly formed handle at one end and being slightly hammered at the other. Caesar was in Britain in 55 and 54 BC, and noted in *De Bello Gallico*, Bk V, Ch. 12, that the British tribes used either bronze or iron bars of standard weight as money. Currency bars were discovered in large quantities in south-west Britain from what is now Worcestershire to Somerset and the Isle of Wight, but very few in the south and south-east where the *Belgae* had introduced coins around 75 BC.

Based on Caesar's statement a very elaborate system of standard weights for bars was worked out with a unit of 11oz (approximately 312g), but clearly not all bars would conform to this standard. The currency bars were used as merchandise in barter trade in exchange for goods such as corn and cattle or were delivered as dues to the head men of settlements in iron-producing districts and subsequently forged into swords or other articles of use by the blacksmith, as indicated by archaeological evidence. It has been claimed that the bars contained too much metal for the manufacture of swords, but the practice of hand-forging meant that the amount of metal could be reduced until the composition was convenient for the grinder who finished the blade.

The brown hematite deposits of the Forest of Dean, with up to 58 per cent of metallic iron content and almost free from impurities such as phosphorus, constituted one of the most important ore resources in Britain. Currency bars analysed from the Forest of Dean area from the first century BC exhibited, as anticipated, only a small amount of phosphorus. When compared with those from more distant areas, and examination of the distribution of currency bars, it was found that four-fifths of them were recovered from within a radius of 40 miles of the Dean ore field. (Information taken from H.R. Schubert, 1957.)

The general lack of specific evidence of iron activity around Dean has tended to encourage the notion that very little iron was produced in that period, but iron ore deposits were being exploited on a small, but widespread, scale. An early Iron Age hillfort at Midsummer Hill, some 14 miles (22.5km) to the north-west of Dean, was excavated by S.C. Stanford

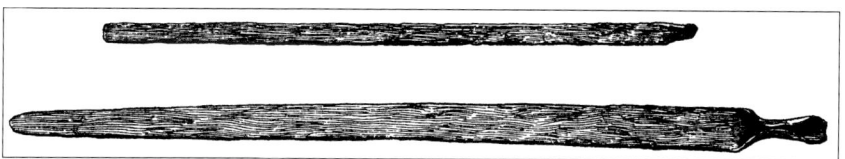

*14* Currency bars, a half unit and one and a half units. *From H.R. Schubert, 1957*

in 1965-70 and iron ores, smelting slags and parts of iron bloom were found and dated to the founding of the settlement in the fifth century BC. The ores were examined and, after comparison with those of other sources, found to be from the Dean hematite (B. Walters, 1992).

Some 3 miles (4.5km) to the east of Ross-on-Wye, and immediately to the west of Bromsash, is a small area marked on the map as 'Aricon'. This indicates roughly the centre of the Iron Age and Romano-British iron-producing area later known as Ariconium. The significance of this settlement remained unknown and undiscovered for over a thousand years until a farmer, clearing scrub from the land prior to cultivation in 1785, discovered Roman artefacts.

Some site investigations during the eighteenth and nineteenth centuries found the remains of stone buildings, a range of artefacts and also inhumation burials. During the twentieth century more evidence was produced of the extent of the settlement and the probable distribution of the various site activities. The most recent investigation by R. Jackson has established the emergence of Ariconium as an elite *Dobunnic* tribal and market centre for their territory, which included what is now south Herefordshire. The economic status of the centre may reasonably be assumed to result from being a production site within the iron industry based around Dean. Proof of their long-range contacts with the south-east comes from findings of a wide range of pottery, mostly early to middle first-century imported wares, and a substantial collection of coins. Much of this evidence can be related to traders in goods from the Continent and south-east having access to the people of this *Dobunnic oppida*. It is likely that the centre would have had a specialist function in providing control over the production and distribution of iron regionally.

In the late Iron Age the settlement would have appeared relatively widespread as there was sufficient room to accommodate agriculture and the various activities of the residents. There would have been a number of family, or extended family, units within which several trades, including ironworking, would have been practised. British craftsmen were very skilled and their use of wheeled transport for some purposes would have resulted in the 'comings and goings' of our ancestors establishing some early roadways, later to be adapted and improved by the Romans.

Archaeological investigation has indicated that the furnaces used for bloomery iron production were very similar throughout the life of Ariconium. They were generally free-standing shaft furnaces with only the

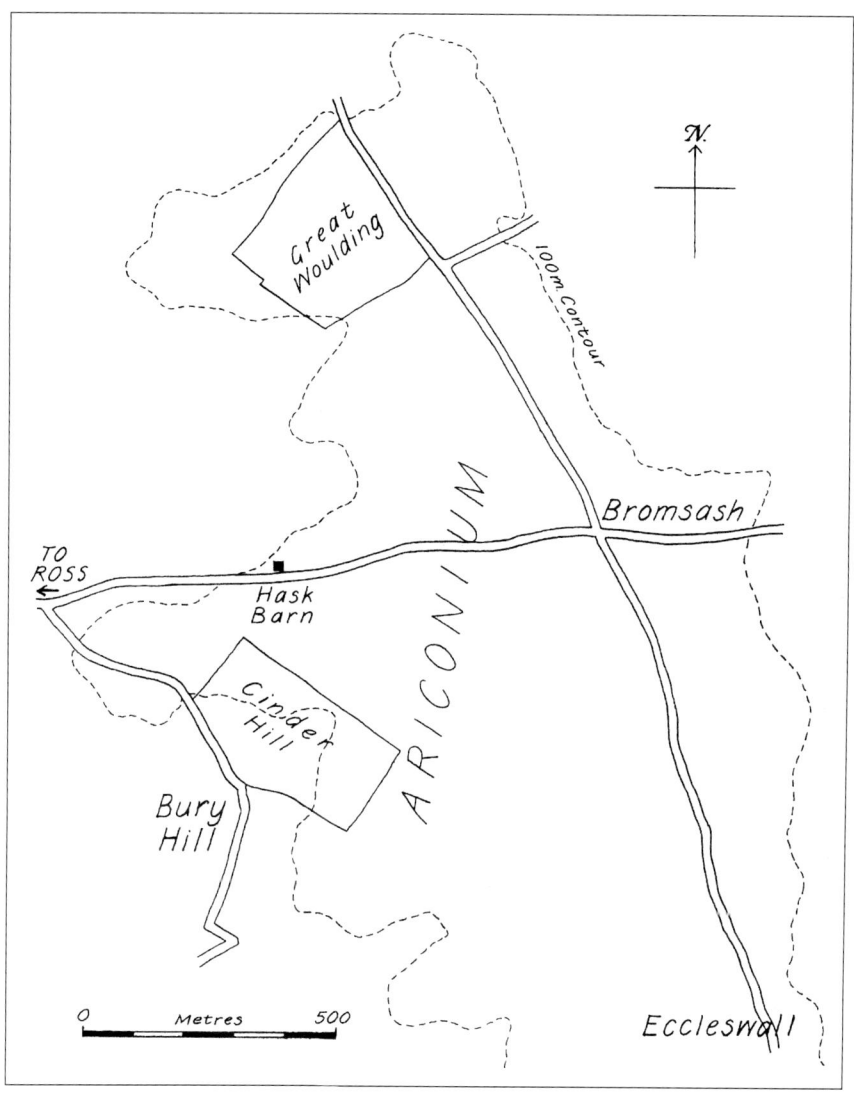

15 Map of Ariconium adjacent to Bromsash

slight remains of the shaft now left within shallow rock-cut depressions. The sizes of these furnaces range from diameters of 12in (0.3m) to 20in (0.5m) and are very similar to furnace remains found at other Dean ironworking sites which sometimes have the tapping pit remains still attached. It is likely that a simple open-sided structure, consisting of a turf and brush covered roof supported on timber posts, would have sheltered the furnaces which generally occupied south- or south-west-facing slopes. There is an argument that placing the furnaces so that they faced the prevailing wind would have utilised good natural draught and possibly obviated the need to force air into the furnaces with bellows.

There are three areas of Ariconium in which evidence of Iron Age activity has been proved. Two ditches were identified when a water pipeline was laid and both produced pottery, briquetage and tapping slag. At the Great Woulding, in the north of the site, are two enclosures argued by Walters and Walters 1989 and Walters 1992 to be early Roman military sites. A more recent assessment of evidence suggests that they were typical of Iron Age and Roman rural settlements. Nevertheless, the possibility that some Roman soldiers may have been present to police the limits of their new territory should not be dismissed. The higher flat ground in the northern part of Ariconium would have afforded good visibility over the Rudhall Brook and surrounding landscape. Both Iron Age ditches investigated on these two enclosures produced quantities of iron slag including material consistent with the use of a tapped furnace, although this was more evident in the southern enclosure. Both appeared to have fallen out of use before the arrival of the Romans but the northern one was re-cut and continued in use until the end of the first century AD. The widest range of Iron Age material came from unstratified finds within the main settlement area and gave proof of the pre-Roman activities of the Iron Age people. No actual remains of a temple or shrine were identified on this site but some probable votive items were found including part of a face pot and three bronze spear heads. Face pot images were not specific but could be related to the smith-deity connected with iron ore and earthy properties which would have been particularly important to the ironworkers of Celtic society. Temples were established at Dean Hall, Coleford and Lydney.

It was known that a Roman imperial monopoly was generally imposed on mineral resources and had been effected on the Wealden iron industry of Sussex and Kent. Rights to extract minerals could also be granted to private entrepreneurial individuals but there is no present evidence of either

imperial or private involvement in the Dean iron industry. It is said that
11 kings made subjection to Claudius at Camulodunum after the arrival
of the Romans in AD 43 (Webster 1993) but only one of their names was
recorded, that of the *Dobunni*. It is assumed that these were the northern
*Dobunni* who occupied the area as far west as Ariconium and what is now
south Herefordshire as they existed in mutual hostility with the southern
*Dobunni* , who were situated further south, on the east side of the Severn
Estuary and were hostile to Rome. Therefore the ironworking centre of
Ariconium and the surrounding territory would have been receptive to
the Roman army and provided them with an iron-producing base which
would be necessary for their future advances westwards.

On the west side of the River Wye the *Silures* were anti-Roman and
fought many guerrilla offensives against them and caused them many
casualties. During the years AD 50-60 massive production of nails, used in
the rapid fort construction in forward bases, probably dominated the iron
supply. It was not until AD 79 that the Welsh tribes were finally subdued, 36
years after the Claudian invasion.

Certainly at Ariconium, and probably at Lydney Park, the Romans
would have met with an existing skilled ironworking force including those
recovering iron ore, charcoal burners, ore smiths and blacksmiths. Roman
army smiths would have accompanied the soldiers and were skilled in
making all the necessary armour and weapons. British craftsmen would
have been capable of producing very good-quality iron and we have seen
in the preface the suggestion that coastal boats were plying their trade some
way up the Severn and feeding the export boats at Hengistbury Head. It
may be reasonable to suggest that Dean iron would have been part of those
export cargoes.

Precise identification of late Iron Age and Roman-period ironworking
sites can, sometimes, be difficult in view of the fact that medieval slags
were frequently spread on the same sites and later mixed with earlier slags,
during recovery for extracting entrapped iron, when blast furnaces came
into use. However, two forms of pottery can provide reasonable evidence
when located in undisturbed stratified layers of slag. The term 'native
ware' is often used to describe dark grey-black cooking pots and storage
jars made by the Britons before, and for a while after, the arrival of the
Romans. They were handmade and thick walled with bead-like rims and
having bodies wider then the diameter of the rim. The second form of
pottery was 'Severn Valley wares' which had a distinctive orange fabric with

a grey core and these were manufactured in several centres throughout the Severn Valley from the first to the fourth centuries AD. There is growing evidence that this pottery was made before the Romans came and is therefore described as 'early Severn Valley ware'. The fabric was usually gritty whereas the pottery made from the second to the fourth centuries was almost free of any inclusions and frequently burnished smooth. A third pottery was Black Burnish ware. This had its origins among the Iron Age *Durotigan* people of Dorset, but was soon being supplied to the Roman army and subsequently became the second most common pottery in the Roman period. The definitively Roman or Romano-British artefacts, such as brooches or coins, found in reasonably undisturbed levels of slag offer a secure basis for dating that layer and its contents to the Roman period. There were four major ironworking centres which fell into the early phase where Roman-period slag covers several acres of land. Ariconium was late Iron Age and Roman with no exhibited slags of later dates. Monmouth dates to the late first and second centuries and lies over deep slag beds. When piles were driven at the Wye Bridge, which connects the town to Dean, slag deposits were found many feet below the present river bed although they could not be dated. Excavations at Granville Street cut through 13ft (4m) of iron-slag layers, which were identified as Roman, and second-century ironworking features, including furnaces, at Spencer's Yard and the Town Wall by Dixton Gate.

Whitchurch overlies very extensive beds of slag with second-century Samian pottery identified 8ft (2.5m) deep in the deposits. In the nineteenth century, while slags were being gathered for reworking to recover more iron from them, deposits up to 10ft (3m) deep were found. Second-century Samian and coarse wares were found in three deep excavations into slag deposits near the village (Bridgewater 1968). It is likely that iron ore for Whitchurch was taken from the nearby Doward hills and the blooms probably forwarded to Monmouth.

The Newent second-century centre, where evidence of industry and settlement covers 117 acres (48ha), was not recorded until 1990 when the Dean Archaeological Group surveyed it by air and on the ground. One of the reasons why this area is interesting is because there is a farm called 'Caerwents' close to the settlement. The 'went' ending to that name and its presence in the name of Newent, has been suggested to mean 'market', 'place' and 'field' and two fields appeared as 'Cinder Pits' on the 1838 tithe map. Pottery finds were similar to Severn Valley wares in form and colour but the fabric was fine sand tempered with grey 'grog' inclusions and, apart from a very rare appearance at Ariconium, was found only at Newent. This site was some 4.5 miles (7km) from the iron ore source at Wigpool, and Gloucester lay about 7.5 miles (12km) to the south-east. Evidence indicates that Newent was a self-contained unit and was active as a 'market' or trading centre in the second century, when domestic demand was at a high level following the surge in iron demand for military purposes in the first century.

It is difficult to assess the manpower content of the production of iron goods but one example will serve to convey some idea of this. At the incompletely constructed Inchtuthil northern Legionary Fortress, occupied from AD 83–86, around one million nails were found. These nails were a very important requirement for the army when establishing their forward forts. It was demonstrated that the manufacture of these nails from worked blooms would have consumed about 50,000 man hours. A reasonable assumption would be that it would take 14 smiths one year to forge these nails (Dr Cleere 1985). The weight of the nails was 7 tonnes so, allowing for the production of average-weight unworked blooms of 30lb (13.6kg), it would have taken upwards of 500 furnace smelts to produce

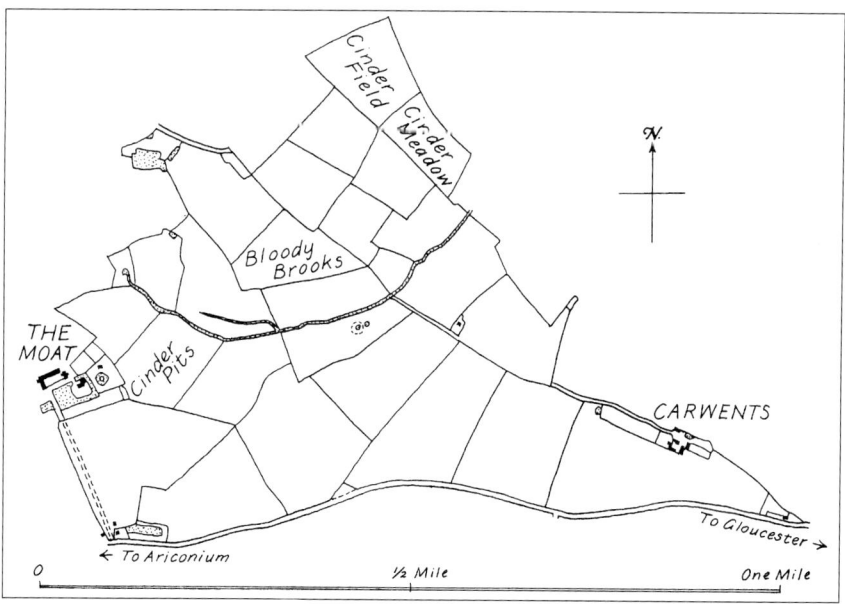

*16* The 'market' area of Newent trading during the second century

the iron needed to forge the one million nails, or more than 7000 two-pound (almost 1kg) forgeable bars. It is likely that the iron required for the northern Roman activities would have been produced in the Weald and shipped up the coast to a northern port.

There is evidence that a small number of local settlements in the area of north Dean were smelting ore for a limited time in the first century AD and we have illustrated the position of these and some production areas east of the River Wye:

### Great Howle
About 3 miles (5km) south-west of Ariconium and nearly 2 miles (3km) west of the ore outcrops at Wigpool. Substantial deposits of bloomery smelting slag and all recovered artefacts were of first-century date, predominantly early Severn Valley ware pottery.

### Ruardean
Almost 1 mile (1.5km) south-east of Great Howle and just over 1 mile (2km) from Wigpool. Quite extensive deposits of bloomery smelting slag found and all pottery finds of early Severn Valley ware.

### Drybrook
Nearly 4 miles (6km) south of Ariconium and situated on a Roman road connecting to Ariconium. It had its own ore outcrops but the scowles, cuts into the rock face to follow iron ore seams, have been filled in. Bloomery smelting slag found beneath field surfaces and all artefacts exclusively of first-century AD date.

### Aston Ingham
Just over 2 miles (3.5km) north-west of Wigpool. A field is strewn with bloomery smelting slag and recovered pottery is entirely first-century Severn Valley ware.

### Huntley
Five miles (8km) from Ariconium with the site lying in the fork of two Roman roads where one branches off to Ariconium. There is a concentration of bloomery slag and pottery finds include first-century Severn Valley ware and some black native ware.

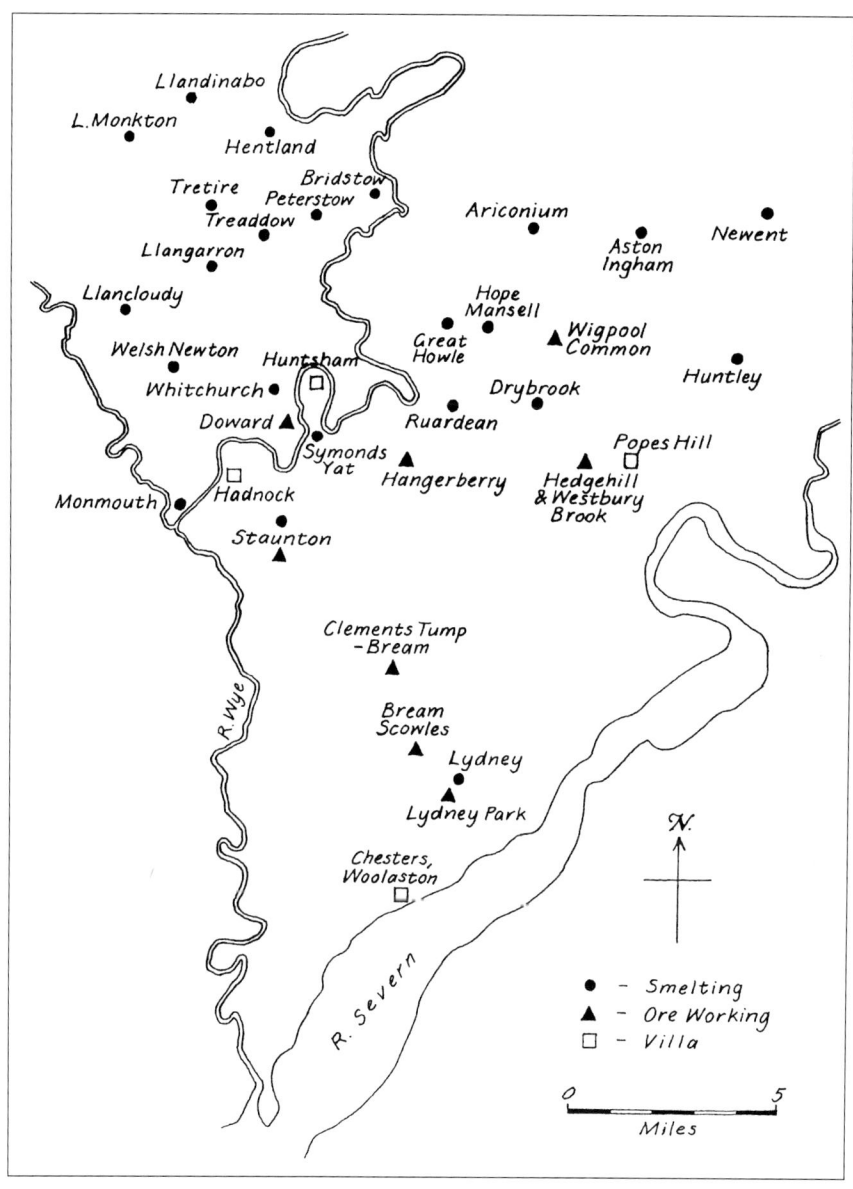

*17* General distribution of ironworking sites in the bloomery period

## Symonds Yat hillfort

A fallen tree lifted a 10ft (3m) long section down to bedrock. First-century Severn Valley wares, black native ware jars and bloomery slag were exposed by this action.

West of the River Wye several iron-producing sites have been located:

## Welsh Newton, Gwenherrion Farm

Smelting slags and furnaces have been identified and pottery, ranging from late first-century to second-century ware, has been recovered.

## Lower Monkton

Several areas of bloomery slag and first-century coarse ware pottery were recovered from the site.

## Lords Wood, Doward Hill

On the lower slopes of the hill a large quantity of bloomery slag was excavated together with first-century jewellery and black native ware pottery. Occupation continued into the second century.

## Tre-Addow

This is a recently discovered site in Hentland parish which was located on an aerial survey by Dean Archaeological Group in 1989. Structural and boundary ditches are accompanied by dense slag deposits from which Romano-British pottery was recovered. This suggests a late first-century activity running through into the second century.

The ore source for these sites was probably the Doward outcrop. It is likely that the ironworking products were directed to Monmouth rather than Ariconium. The extensive smelting areas of Whitchurch are only just over 0.5 miles (1km) from the Doward and Monmouth is some 2.5 miles (4km) to the south.

The word 'villa' can be a little misleading as it was applied to residential buildings of the Roman era ranging from farmhouses to those of higher status. Those of the early period were probably farmhouses and some of them were later developed to a higher quality or purpose built for managers of commercial and industrial activities including iron production. Two can be identified in the first to second century where they followed Iron Age settlements and are discussed in the following paragraphs.

In the loop of the River Wye at Huntsham aerial photographs from a Dean Archaeological Group survey revealed two Iron Age enclosures. Subsequent investigation found abundant evidence of bloomery iron-smelting and native pottery from the middle of the first century. A villa was built adjacent to the earlier enclosure and investigation produced pottery, dating to the mid-second century, of Romano-British type. The villa appeared to have only a modest type of luxury about it but flourished later in the second century.

Below the Little Doward hillfort, but on the opposite side of the River Wye, lies the site of Hadnock villa which had its own road link to the Mitcheldean to Monmouth road and is just over 1 mile (2km), upstream from that town. The site was discovered by fieldwalkers from Monmouth Archaeological Society and they found heavy deposits of iron slag in the area. Pottery finds of black native ware sets an early date for this site. Romano-British pottery found here gives a probable villa date of the second century.

The urgent need for the production of iron for military purposes from AD 50 onwards had undoubtedly resulted in the increase of small smelting sites but some seemed to have declined during the later years of the first century. This was possibly because they had moved closer to the main

*18* Iron Age farmstead at Huntsham. © *Mark Walters DAG aerial survey*

*19* Romano-British iron mining site, The Mount, Lydbrook. © *Mark Walters DAG aerial survey*

*20* Crop marks of iron-mining scowles, Double View, Littledean. © *Mark Walters DAG aerial survey*

production areas of Ariconium, Monmouth and Coleford. In the second century the development of urban centres, such as Gloucester, Cirencester and Caerwent, would have resulted in an emphasis on a far wider range of iron products for domestic purposes and tested the skills of the smiths.

At Ariconium iron production which would have moved from the more northern area of the site to the vicinity of the Hask Barn where N.P. Bridgewater excavated an area of 84 x 72ft (25.6 x 22m) in 1963. He found evidence of six furnaces, primary smithing, a charcoal store and some coal samples which he dated as ranging from before AD 125 up to the end of the second century. Another area of ironworking lies to the south of Hask Barn at Cinder Hill where most surface finds are consistently second century. There are more than 30 acres (12ha) here covered by slag spreads and ironworking debris from the second century.

The areas of Monmouth previously described were very productive in the second century and watching briefs by Monmouth Archaeological Society in the Monnow Street area and the rescue excavation at the former Glendower Street School by the Dean Archaeological Group, proved the abundance of iron-smelting at that time. The wide range of pottery assemblages recovered consistently comprised second-century wares.

# 3

# THIRD CENTURY TO THE TWELFTH CENTURY

The increased production of iron in the late second and into the third centuries coincided with the establishment of western seaways to service Roman garrisons on the west coast. At Ariconium the northern ironworking areas were deserted but continued demand was signified by the creation of a new smelting area to the south-west which continued in production into the fourth century. The ironworking area of Monmouth moved out of the southern suburbs onto the other side of the Monnow, and alongside the road to Usk at Overmonnow. Other sites, close to the mines at Coleford, were in production and new sites appeared at Park Farm, Lydney and Chesters. Some minor sites along the shores of the Severn Estuary also produced ironworking activities: Hills Flats, Oldbury Flats, Rumney Great Wharf and Severn House Farm, some of which may have had Iron Age origins (Allen and Fulford 1987).

Around the middle of the third century some villa sites began smelting and smithing activities. There would have been a general requirement for a limited amount of ironworking, probably by their own smiths, and some would have carried out this work within gaps in the arable farming year, say between sowing and harvest. In modern times some village blacksmiths' shops survived only to the mid-twentieth century and then began to disappear as the requirements of the public changed. The blacksmiths used to repair agricultural machinery, make and repair domestic tools and fabricate utilitarian domestic items, but their redundancy began when agricultural machinery became large and complex and domestic items were mass-produced or fell out of use. Villas at Woolaston, Hadnock and

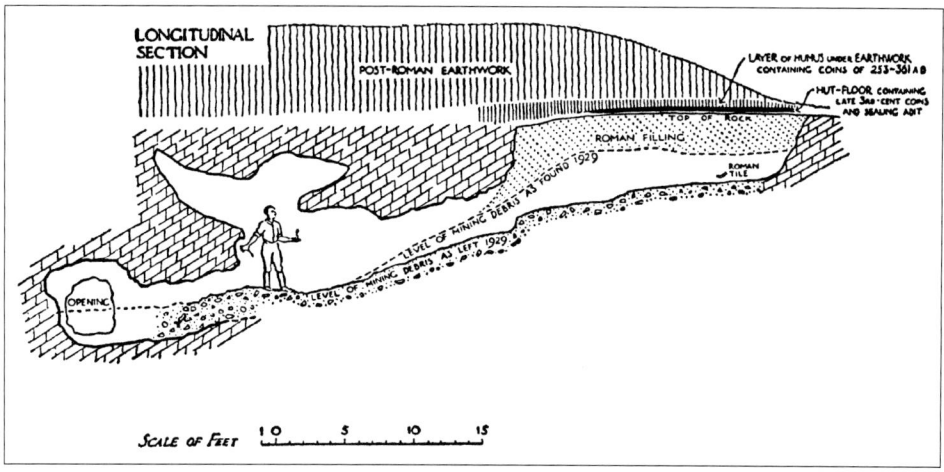

LONGITUDINAL SECTION

POST-ROMAN EARTHWORK

LAYER of HUMUS UNDER EARTHWORK CONTAINING COINS OF 253-361 AD

HUT-FLOOR CONTAINING LATE 3RD-CENT COINS AND SEALING ADIT

ROMAN FILLING

TOP OF ROCK

ROMAN TILE

LEVEL OF MINING DEBRIS AS FOUND 1929

LEVEL OF MINING DEBRIS AS LEFT 1929

OPENING

SCALE OF FEET   1 0      5      10      15

21 Lydney Iron Mine. *After R.E.M. and T.V.Wheeler, 1932*

Popes Hill have yielded quite high deposits of slag, sufficient to indicate that they probably produced iron which would have been surplus to their requirements and possibly traded that for produce which they did not raise themselves. The land adjacent to Popes Hill, for example, is suitable for livestock rearing but not arable farming, so they would have needed to trade for grain and other arable produce. There is a limited amount of good arable land surrounding Huntsham villa, in a loop of the River Wye, but a reassessment of Bridgewater's excavation there suggests that they may have malted barley and produced liquor, in some quantity, to distribute via river transport. (*Transactions of the Woolhope Naturalists' Field Club*, Taylor E. Vol. XLVIII, 1995, Part II.)

At Chesters villa, Woolaston, M. Fulford was excavating from 1988-90 and revealed an industrial building with 16 bays, measuring 53ft 8in x 27ft 6in (16.5 x 8.2m). It was of post-built construction on two parallel rows of pad-stones. Several shaft-type furnaces were confirmed together with an ore-crushing unit. The ironworking phase, based on limited pottery evidence, was calculated to have terminated by around the mid-third century (Fulford, M. 1991). Dense layers of slag had been deposited nearby to form a landing stage to the estuary inlet.

It is possible that an ironworking phase to the mid-third century may be allocated to the Hadnock villa and it could possibly have extended later, but there is no end dating for the slag deposits.

Some limited smelting and smithing took place at Park Farm villa, Lydney, although again the slag deposits have not been dated. The iron mining phase at Lydney Park might well be associated with the villa. R.E. M. and T.V. Wheeler (1932) dated the mining phase as middle to later third century. By no means has all of the mining activity been dated as a temple site is overlaying the complex mining system. The existence of the mines may be somewhat remarkable as available ore outcrops exist as far as the major scowles at Bream, which are less than 1.25 miles (2km) north-west of the temple site. Of course, it is possible that the earliest of the outcrops in this area had already been exhausted by second-century over-production. It is possible that the Lydney tunnel mines produced more ore than was ever smelted at the Park Farm villa and, if this was so, then the Chesters villa could well have drawn its ore from Lydney.

It appears that, Lydney apart, most of the ore was now being drawn from the ore outcrops south of Coleford, possibly from the Noxon area. Third-century coins have been found alongside the ore outcrops in Scowles village, and at Perrygrove scowles upwards of 3000 mid-third-century coins were found in 1849, both official and 'barbarous' radiate copies. These were found hidden in jars pushed into a crack in the quarried-out scowles

*22* Lydney Temple site. Aerial view of the excavations. *Reprinted by kind permission of the Frank Harris Collection*

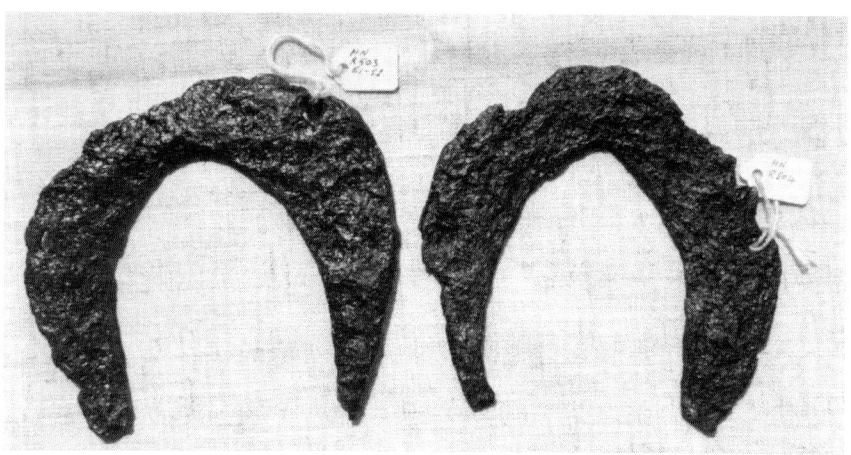

23 Two Romano-British horseshoes recovered from High Nash, Coleford. *Alf Webb*

which confirms that that particular scowle had been exhausted and no future operations would disturb the cache!

Sometime around the early third century a remarkable new building was constructed for the community of iron workers at Coleford, High Nash. It was a timber-built temple of considerable proportions and was approximately 46ft (14m) wide and possibly 85ft (26m) long, including an apse. It is reasonably certain that the temple was constructed during the years of decline in the iron industry but this might have concentrated the minds of the Britons on intercession with their gods, who had been so benevolent towards them for so long. Part of the foundations of the temple had been destroyed by a new road laid to an industrial estate in 1985 and Dean Archaeological Group undertook a salvage operation which revealed the rest of the temple plan. Among the dedicatory deposits discovered during the work were two iron horseshoes which reflected the relationship between the Britons and the horse. Many 'Celtic' coins had featured the horse and the *Dobunnic* coinage had carried a triple-tailed horse.

Towards the end of the third century there would have been a surplus of labour in skilled crafts compared with the early years of the century, and in 297 the new emperor, Constantius, drew 'artificers' to restore the important city of Autun in Gaul.

The High Nash rescue excavations provided evidence of a modestly flourishing settlement throughout the fourth century. In the mid-third century the temple, and an adjacent shrine, were demolished and the foundation trenches filled with silt. The trenches contained many fragments of fourth-century pottery, notably Black Burnished wares and many Oxfordshire flagons. Subsequently a new shrine was built on the site of the earlier temple but this was later replaced, in the late fourth century, by what could only have been an altar, set beneath a covering supported by posts on pad-stones. It is reasonably certain that the site functioned into the early years of the fifth century.

The first Roman-period smelting site to be excavated by the Dean Archaeological Group in 1987 was at Barnfield, Hangerbury. The field, 650ft (198m) above sea-level, contains three roughly circular areas of concentrated slag and furnace debris, each about 65ft (20m) in diameter. Excavation on one of them revealed slag to a depth of about 14in (35cm). A shaft-type furnace had been constructed from clay extracted from an adjacent pit. A piece of sandstone had been used as the furnace base on which the shaft, with an internal width of 10.5in (27cm), had been built. The slag had tapped from the furnace into the clay extraction pit and three distinctly different smelts were to be observed. The first two flowed into the pit after which the pit had been filled with debris. The third flowed across the top of the pit.

The stratified pottery sherds were all commonly produced Severn Valley wares and therefore not closely datable, but a nearby surface find of a Centenionalis of Constantius II with a Christogram reverse and minted in Trier in 353 very strongly suggests a mid- to later fourth-century date for the smelting. That dating is substantiated by another nearby surface find, a rim sherd of fourth-century Oxfordshire colour-coated mortarium.

Not far from the smelting site, on the summit of Hangerbury Hill, are iron ore outcrop scowles, clearly the source of the ore. The slag remains, covering half to three-quarters of an acre (0.2023-0.3034ha), have not been widely spread by ploughing and may represent former banks of 20,000-25,000 tons (20,320-25,400 tonnes) in total. The appearance of this smelting and primary smithing site so late in the fourth century may well be further evidence that the major ore outcrops were by now exhausted or on the point of being so. Beside a trackway, in a neighbouring field, which leads to the Lydbrook Valley and the Wye a typical Roman-type 2.5lb (1.1340kg) forgeable iron bar, of square section, was found. Production may well have been in excess of local needs and it is probable that some iron was being shipped away by river.

Across the valley from Hangerbury, at Cowmeadow Farm, in English Bicknor parish, on another ridge, a small Roman-period smelting site was located. A partly worked billet was found, the shaped part being of square section, close to a large circular spread of slag. Surface pottery was again fourth century and included an Oxfordshire colour-coated mortarium rim, and a rim of a pewter dish was also found. Hangerbury would have been the ore source for this site.

Both these sites were new, although Hangerbury had been occupied in the first century AD. The possible continuity link between the two might have been the probable 'villa' site at Lydbrook overlooking the Wye which seems to have survived the centuries. Among its latest pottery was the almost ubiquitous Oxfordshire colour-coated wares.

The temple site at Dean Hall was still flourishing in the fourth century and a coin of Magnentius was sealed beneath the latest phase, and this may coincide with the phase two, reduced-size temple, at High Nash, Coleford. With the exception of the possible villa site at Popes Hill, none of the ironworking areas around Littledean have yet been dated within the Roman period although, in 1992, slag fragments from a late Roman road surface were excavated within 82yds (75m) of the temple.

Wheeler dated the Lydney Temple complex to the 360s but more recent research has led to the belief that it may have been late third or early fourth century AD. Up to date findings indicate that Lydney was a key port in the later Roman period and, by inference, a supply depot. The coin sequence for the temple ends with Honorius so the use of the building survived well into the fifth century, which is remarkable for a pagan temple.

The potential Stock Farm villa at Clearwell has not been excavated but might possibly be the home of a mining administrator who would have been in residence as long as ore was being extracted from the adjacent mines or others nearby. All that can be said at present is that a fourth-century occupation is indicated by Oxfordshire and Nene Valley colour-coated wares being recovered from trial excavations close to the villa. Substantial local evidence indicates that although Oxfordshire white ware mortaria were reaching the region in the third century, the colour-coated wares were not distributed west of the Severn, in any quantity, until the fourth century, where they are found in the very latest Roman contexts.

The Chesters villa at Woolaston was excavated in the 1930s. A break in continuity was seen between the first period, in the early fourth century, and the second period which began sometime after 320. A platform feature on higher ground just to the north of the building was interpreted as a 'lighthouse' to guide shipping into the Pill around the submerged

Guscar Rocks. It was placed in period two (fourth century) and the latest coin in the sequence was of Gratian, minted in the 370s. The main building, revealed by a Dean Archaeological Group aerial survey in 1989, is unexcavated. That it was heavily buttressed and therefore possibly multi-storey in its latest phase is discernible from the cropmarks. The 1930 excavation had examined the baths and it would be interesting to know if the same sequence of operations were reflected in the main building. Evidence suggests that there was also a break in construction of the main building during which there was no occupation. No ironworking on the villa site has yet been dated to the fourth century.

At the nearby Boughspring villa the mid-fourth century saw major developments when the earlier winged-corridor villa was converted into a baths system and a new multi-storey building was erected in front of it on a platform. Only a small amount of pottery was available for a report put together by Joyce Pullinger in 1990 but Nene Valley and mainly Oxfordshire colour-coated wares were again present. Some small amount of ironworking took place near the villa but its precise location is not known.

Hadnock villa, Huntsham villa and Park Farm villa at Lydney were all functioning in the fourth century but we have no excavated evidence of fourth-century ironworking.

24 Chesters villa, Woolaston, showing the large Roman building site previously unknown. © *Mark Walters DAG aerial survey*

From around AD 300 much work was carried out on country houses, from improvements to modest houses to the creation of grand mansions. Within Dean it is only the Woolaston and Boughspring villas which attracted improvements while most of the numerous villas east of the Severn demonstrate fourth-century improvements. The effect of this upsurge in development did not appear to result in an increase in iron production in Dean but it did help to sustain the industry at a level it achieved by the later third century after the slump.

During 1991/2 several small fourth-century ironworking sites have been identified close to the Severn, especially in the parish of Awre and close to Blakeney. These sites are far from any known villas and it is possible that a villa remains to be discovered. At Viney Hill, in Awre parish, there is a Chester Leye field name and Romano-British pottery sherds have been found but no traces of an occupation area. Datable pottery finds on all of these sites are late third/fourth century with Oxfordshire wares consistently being found.

Around 367 there were reports to the authorities in Rome that Britain had suffered severe attacks from barbarians which had reduced the provinces of Britain to the verge of ruin. It is further recorded that forces were despatched to repel the invaders, which had presumably been achieved by 369. There is no obvious archaeological evidence around Dean for any barbarian attacks. Even across the Severn, the prominent Frocester villa was found to be thriving at the time recorded for the attacks. Neither was any evidence found at the Boughspring or Chesters villas, both of which seemed to thrive in the 360s.

In recent years several substantial coin hordes have been found in Dean. At Oldcroft, nearly 2 miles (3km) from Lydney and alongside the Dean Road, 3333 coins and some silver bullion were found in 1972/3. Some were of Constantius II with the latest being of Julian II and it was judged that the deposit had been made in or after 359. During 1991 a second hoard was excavated by Dean Archaeological Group close by the deposition spot of the first hoard. Coins were mostly of Constantius II and had originally been hidden in a dry-stone field wall running parallel to the Dean Road. This deposition was held to be after 354 (M.J. Walters, 1991). At High Woolaston, nearly 1 mile (1.5km) north-west of Chesters villa, some 250 coins were discovered in 1887. At Bishopswood, Walford, on a hillside, over 800ft (250m) above the Wye, over 17,000 coins were found; 16,070 of them were minted during the period 330-5 and the latest coin was dated to 348.

There is no known Roman occupation site within several miles of this hoard but the site was taken into private ownership which made it difficult to investigate further.

Fourth-century ironworking continued at Ariconium and Monmouth but both fell into a period of decline and production ceased by around AD 350. By comparison some of the villa sites and higher-status centres, such as the temple complex at Lydney, were obviously achieving maximum production at this time but, by the late fourth century, iron production seems to have virtually ceased. This must have reflected the decline of demand from the wider economy at the end of the fourth century. It is also likely that the iron ore sources at Wigpool and the Doward had been virtually exhausted by this time.

Few dictates of the rulers would have directly affected the working Britons but one series, although short in duration, was aimed directly at their religious beliefs. In 353 Constantius II assumed control of Britain following the 'not unusual differences' between the sons of Constantine, who had given Britain a long period of stability. However, Constantius was aggressively Christian and ordered the banning of the Celtic religion and the closure of all pagan temples on pain of death! His 'enforcer', Paulus, had a well-earned reputation for his part in tortures, imprisonments and death sentences. However, the decree was more effective in urban centres than in the countryside where forests, rivers, streams and springs were natural visible images of the Celtic spirit. The situation eased in 355 when Julian, a cousin of Constantius, was appointed Caesar over Britain. Julian had an interest in history, religion and tradition and a much broader attitude to his territory. As an aside, it is interesting to note that Britain's agriculture was obviously healthy at this time for in 359 Julian sent 600 ships from Britain to carry and supply corn to the lower Rhine armies!

At some time during the last two decades of the fourth century we know that Chesters and Boughspring villas were abandoned and left to crumble. It is also accepted that the Romans surrendered their administrative hold on Britain at a time when it seems that some saw that economic decline would result in eventual disaster and moved away from Dean.

Towards the end of the Roman presence in the area of the Forest and the surrounding countryside, as the military numbers had been greatly reduced, the local population continued to produce food and farm. Farming had developed with the Roman influence and the number of corn driers found in farmsteads is an indication of climatic conditions at that time. Britons worked hard producing food to support themselves and the Romano-British elite, in addition to the payment of taxes to the hierarchy. So, when the Romans departed around 409, most of the population would have felt some relief from the burden of taxation and were perfectly capable of supporting themselves. The so-called 'Dark Ages' is a period in which it is said that no records of iron production exist but it would obviously have continued, as it did many centuries later, at a level which would have supported the requirements of the local communities.

The Saxons did not impose their presence until the late sixth century following the battle of Dyrham. For almost two centuries following the departure of the Romans, the people of Dean and the surrounding area must have enjoyed a period of peaceful self-sufficiency. Woodland renewed itself and nature began to claim the exhausted and deserted ore outcrops. The slag heaps were to remain for more than a thousand years as testimony to the exploitation of resources during the Romano-British period. (Information from B. Walters, 1992.)

Several attempts have been made to establish the quantity of ore which would have been processed in a given period. The Wigpool outcrops were almost certainly the source of iron ore for Ariconium and Newent and it is suitable to use these centres to obtain an estimate of ore processed at both during the Roman period. It has been estimated that about 475,000 tonnes of ore could have been smelted at both sites during the second century. First-century ironworking at Ariconium produced a concentrated slag cover of 3 acres (1.25ha) which would equate to a slag heap of 175,000 tonnes. So the overall extraction of iron ore from Wigpool in the Roman period, when we equate the quantity of slag to equal that of iron ore, would have been around 650,000 tonnes.

It is often stated that Ariconium was situated in an important position on the Roman XIII Itinerary between Gloucester and Monmouth. It is probable, however, that the Roman 'Road Atlas' was positioned on some previous Iron Age roadways which were upgraded and obviously improved. The distribution of iron production centres around the perimeter of the Forest might possibly have been dictated by pre-Roman control over ore sources, mining and distribution. Transport for the finished iron product would have been important and it is notable that the Forest area was provided with an extensive road system, parts of which offered access to the River Severn or the River Wye, which were also part of the transport provision. Possibly the major consideration in placing the iron-smelting centres would be the availability of charcoal fuel because it is far more bulky than ore or finished products and, traditionally, the ore had been taken to the charcoal source. Evidence seems to point to the fact that Lydney was an important port serving the Severn.

Ariconium was a staging post on the road system between Gloucester and Monmouth and the foundation remains of a number of 'high status' stone buildings were discovered on the site, one of which may have been the *mansio*. After the closing of a major part of the settlement and the probable appearance of dereliction, travellers may well have used the central road from Gloucester to Monmouth. Archaeological records of the numerous indications of the former extent of the Ariconium settlement confirm that it was a major establishment which fell into disuse for well over a thousand years and was only rediscovered when neglected land was being brought into use to feed a growing population (J. Thirsk 1985). Farmer Merrick said that he had dug out 'vast' quantities of stone and numerous artefacts and his plough constantly struck ruins. Of course there are no records, but this period was the start of the decay of archaeological evidence of our early history.

In the early part of the eleventh century Canute, the Scandinavian king of England, was the first to utilise forest areas as royal hunting grounds and Edward the Confessor shared his love of the sport. William the Conqueror increased the areas of forest and established a 'forest law'. Because the Court moved around the country it was necessary to have the provision of food in appropriate places so, when the Court visited Gloucester, Dean forest became the royal forest. It was not until 1970 that Queen Elizabeth II decreed the abandonment of royal forests.

*Domesday Book* is fairly silent respecting the mines, iron works and miners of the Forest. We learn from it that Edward the Confessor (1003–66) was accustomed to demanding from the citizens of Gloucester, 'thirty-six dicres of iron and a hundred elongated iron rods for bolts for the king's ships'. A dicre is a measure of 10 and the quantity mentioned here would shoe 180 horses. The drawn rods would probably make around 10,000 nails. Less than a hundred years later we are told that 16s worth of iron was sent, in 1158, to Woodstock by the king's order, besides 8s worth more for repairs to his palace. An observation of Geraldus, describing the tour he made through Wales in 1188, speaks of the 'noble Forest of Dean, by which Gloucester was amply supplied with iron and venison' (*Iron Making in the Forest of Dean,* Nicholls 1866).

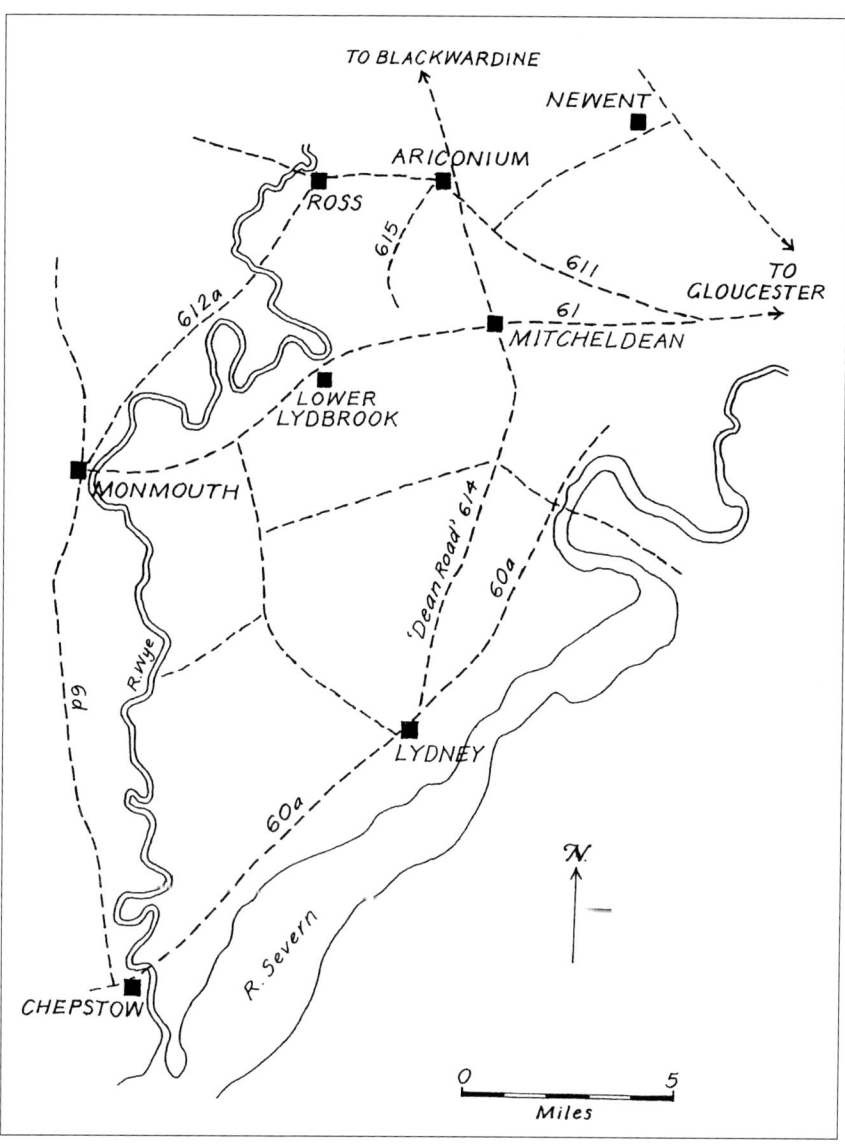

TO BLACKWARDINE

NEWENT

ARICONIUM

ROSS

615

612a

611

TO GLOUCESTER

61

MITCHELDEAN

LOWER LYDBROOK

MONMOUTH

'Dean Road' 614

60a

R. Wye

6d

LYDNEY

60a

60a

R. Severn

N.

CHEPSTOW

0          5
Miles

25 Layout of roads in the Roman period, with those investigated by Ivan Margary given his appropriate numbers

There are, however, some hints in *Domesday Book* where a few words indicate that the iron industry did exist: *Ferrum* = iron, *Bloma* = bloom, *Minariae* = iron mines, *Ferrariae* or *Ferri fabricae* = forges or bloomeries, *Ferrarii* = smiths and *Ferrum carrucis* = ironwork for ploughs. In addition, two further entries are of interest:

> In the manor belongs a hide of land which, in the time of King Edward the Confessor, used to render 50 blooms of iron and six salmon.

The place referred to is probably in the Newland Valley near the Scowles at Coleford. The other entry is that:

> Turstin Fitz Rolf held six hides at Alwintune and rendered 20 blooms of iron.

It is thought that this place is between The Slaughter, on the south-east of the River Wye below Lords Wood on the Doward, and Hillersland, almost 1 mile (1.5km) away to the east. It is known that the Saxons were ardent agriculturalists and cleared much land around the forest including areas where iron ore existed and wherever good land could be won.

Parts of the country were devastated by internal fighting prior to the Norman Conquest and much depredation was caused by the following subjugation of the country by William and his Normans. In 1104 the *Anglo-Saxon Chronicle* relates that:

> nor is it easy to tell of the misery the land was enduring in these times, through various and manifold injustices and taxes, which never lessened or ceased; and always wherever the king went [King Henry] he was through his court plundering his wretched folk thoroughly, very often with burning and manslaughter.

Anarchy marked the reign of Stephen, the last Norman king of England (1135-54), and the garrisons of his castles lived off the surrounding land and their forays extended outwards until the castles stood in a large area of devastated land. However, after the ravages of the occupation, the south-west, extending from northern Somerset across the Forest of Dean and into Herefordshire, regained its importance quite early and retained that status well into the fourteenth century. Whilst *Domesday Book* was being compiled the Benedictine Abbey of Glastonbury, in Somerset, was producing a considerable amount of iron for they had eight smiths, compared with six in the city of Hereford. These smiths obtained their ore from Pucklechurch in Gloucestershire which belonged to the Abbey. Iron works referred to in the late eleventh century were mainly on land held by the king's baronial followers. Alvington, south-west of Lydney, produced a large number of blooms of iron and was held by Thurston, son of Rolf, a baron from Normandy.

Iron works recorded at later dates were also first possessed by lay owners of the Norman nobility before being granted to monastic orders, which was quite significant in the Forest of Dean area and the valley of the River Wye. Early in the twelfth century Baderon of Monmouth had one forge at Osbaston, west of Monmouth, and three others on the River Wye near Monmouth. He gave the three forges in the Wye Valley to the Benedictine Priory of Monmouth but retained the Osbaston one for himself. Milo, Earl of Hereford, who died in 1143, owned a forge near St Briavels which he granted to one of the earliest Cistercian Abbeys in England, founded at Tintern on the Wye, in 1131. The first charter granted to the Abbey of Flaxley by Henry II whilst Duke of Normandy (and previous to 1154 the year he came to the throne) specifies an iron works at Elton, near Westbury, on the eastern side of the Forest. His second charter, when king, is more explicit and describes 'an iron forge, free and quit, with as free liberty to work as any of his forges in demesne', showing that he possessed several at that time.

The acquisition of iron works by Cistercian Abbeys, such as Flaxley and Tintern, almost immediately after their foundation, reveals an eagerness to secure mining rights and to develop the production of iron, which is equally characteristic of the Cistercian houses founded in the same period in the north of England. There, some of the mines and iron works had also belonged to lay owners before the Order acquired them. (Information from Schubert and Nicholls.)

The *Pipe Rolls* gives us some clear information of financial conditions and also provides evidence of the productivity of the Forest ironworkers in the latter part of the twelfth century. In 1165 arms were sent from Dean of the order of 60 axes, 70 picks and 6 hoes with 18d. of rope. In 1167 two barrels of arrows and siege engines were sent to Henry II at a cost of 116s. For the invasion of Ireland in 1171 by the same king and Strongbow, the Earl of Pembroke, William de Rudes was paid £1 5s 6d for shoes and nails for the king's horses, while Prince Henry, who stayed at home, received seven plates and a cauldron for the price of 11s 6d. During the same operation Simon Croom, a military man of Warwick, supplied 2000 picks and 1000 spades, almost certainly made from Forest iron.

Among several items mentioned in 1172 are 50,000 nails for 43s 6d, 60,000 nails for 53s 6d, 50,000 big nails for 45s 10d and 5000 big nails for 6s 8d. In the same year the king paid 22s 11d for 100 axes to be sent to Ireland. The Bailiff of Gloucester paid 17s 10d. for 60,000 nails and £5 for 2000 iron spade heads. For the siege of Leicester in 1173 the Sheriff paid 33s 4d for 10,000 arrows and some siege engines. It is evident that an appreciable difference in the size of the two types of nails must account for the difference in price, and that munitions manufacture and mass-production are not modern innovations.

Twelve years later Pagan of St Briavels paid 5 marks (1 mark being equivalent to 6s 8d) for seizing of a forge and one mark rent of same, whilst Aernulf of Blakeney paid 62s 8d for his forge. In 1188 iron for the use of the king in his journey to Jerusalem cost £8, 16s 3d. In 1191 the Sheriff paid £33 18s for 50,000 horseshoes, with double calcins, and £100 for iron for the king's ships (from I. Cohen).

# THE THIRTEENTH AND FOURTEENTH CENTURIES

Fears regarding the excessive demands for timber for converting to charcoal were borne out in 1216 when royal control of iron forges resulted in John de Monmouth being authorised to control them by deciding where forges would be allowed. In 1217 Henry III ordered that all private forges should be removed with only six exceptions. From 1244 permission to mine iron ore was regulated by the Crown so there are many records of rights but no information on the equipment used. The abbots of Flaxley had been allowed to cut two oaks weekly for their forge, but they were given a grant in 1258 of 872 acres (352ha) of what is now known as Abbots Wood, a privilege they lost at the Dissolution of the Monasteries by Henry VIII (1509-47). Despite the problems caused by the vacillation of the Crown regarding timber usage the thirteenth and fourteenth centuries saw great activity in the iron industry and ironworking was the main occupation.

The alternating orders and countermands naturally raised difficulties, so we find a number of claims put forward in respect of the claims of ironworkers. In 1274 Sir Hervey de Caduris claimed the right to a forge, the adjudicators being the Sheriff and Sir William de Blund, the Deputy Constable. The forge was valued at 48 marks and in 1276 he was granted 500 marks in quit claim.

The importance of St Briavels, in the early medieval period, cannot be underestimated. For much of the early warfare, the Barons' war and the campaigns against Wales, it was the king's armament depot, in fact Edward I called it his 'Great Arsenal'. It was noted for its massive production of quarrels, the square-headed arrows or bolts used with a crossbow, in the thirteenth century which could have amounted to well over a million. Hector Cole, a blacksmith specialising in replica weapons and tools, supplied an article for *Dean Archaeology No 5* of 1992, in which the tools are illustrated. He estimated that one arrowsmith would be capable of forging 120 bodkin heads in a 12-hour day or 2600 heads in one year based on 300 working days a year. This meant that for St Briavels to produce 50,000 quarrels in the year 1257, 14 arrowsmiths, three bar forgers and six grinder pointers would be required – a workforce of 23. Added to this would be packers, apprentices, bellows boys and others bringing in the raw materials so the in-house staff would have to be 50-strong and this does not include those obtaining the ore, charcoal burners, arrowshaft makers, the fletchers and transport to and from the site. Orders to St Briavels ranged in their thousands and the royal castles in Wales and the Marches were supplied on 9 or 10 occasions.

In the thirteenth century, England became a state dominated by clerks and the written word. Governmental commands and every expenditure were recorded. The information survives in the *Close Rolls*, the *Liberate Rolls*, the *Minister's* and *Receiver's Accounts*, the *Exchequer Papers of the King's Remembrancer*, the *Treasury of Receipt Papers* and, from 1277, the *Welsh Rolls*. Other evidence is contained in *Brut Y Tywysogyon*, or the *Chronicle of the Princes*. Most of the evidence has been 'calendared', that is indexed into date order with brief details of the contents.

Iron mining took place in Dean throughout the first to the fourth centuries AD, but the activity was probably reduced until the Normans intensified the industry. Certainly before 1244 miners were allowed to win ore (mine ore), subject to dues in cash or kind being paid, either to the 'foresters-of-fee' in the nine bailiwicks of Dean, or to the constable of St Briavels castle on behalf of the king. By the thirteenth century the miners were a relatively 'free' and privileged class. It has been estimated that some hundreds of thousands of tons of ore and cinders had been re-dug for re-smelting in the thirteenth to the sixteenth centuries.

The order to the constable of St Briavels Castle to send 6000 quarrels to Montgomery in 1223 is the first recorded with a similar order placed the following year, when he had to deliver to Ralph FitzNicholas all the quarrels he had caused to be made. But it is an order made on 2 November 1228 that really starts the story of John Malemort. The king (Henry III) notified the bailiff of St Briavels that three workmen were being sent to assist in the making of quarrels. They were William the Smith, who was to be paid 5d a day, his brother John de Malemort, to be paid 4d a day and William the Fletcher, who also was to receive 4d a day.

The bailiff was to pay the wages and supply the necessary iron and charcoal. The Sheriffs of Gloucestershire and Herefordshire were given orders to supply feathers for William the Fletcher's use in an order dated 2 July 1229. On 16 November that year, the two Malemorts were promised an increase of 2.5d a day, and William the Fletcher 1.5d a day, provided 100 quarrels were made each day.

In November 1229 and again in May 1230, the bailiff had orders to provide charcoal and iron, and a building in which the Malemorts could work. Whether there were some family problems shortly after is not known, but on 4 January 1232 only John Malemort was named in an order to raise his pay to 10.5d a day. On 17 December 1232 the constable was again ordered to supply iron, charcoal, lard, bran, barrels, wood, a grindstone and a building for John Malemort to work in. He was still required to make 100 quarrels a day.

Those instructions called for iron (*ferri*), which would have been supplied as bloom, a spongy mass of ferrous oxide and silica. On site this would be reheated and hammered into a solid block, turning bloom into wrought iron, a continuous network of iron grains interspersed with a few stringers of slag which had not been eliminated. It was an extremely wasteful process as the waste could contain anything up to 80 per cent iron content.

The charcoal was supplied by the Forest charcoal burners, whilst the lard (*iard*) would have been available from the many pigs kept in the Forest. After working the wrought iron into quarrel heads, they would be plunged, still warm, into the lard to stop rust. The bran was the husks separated from flour, and quarrels were packed in barrels in the bran so that edges were not blunted in transit. Wood was no problem. John of Monmouth in 1237, constable of St Briavels, with the foresters-of-fee and verderers was told to enquire in what places eight movable forges could be placed within the Forest with the least damage to make use of maple, thorn, hazel and dead wood. Oak, beech, ash and chestnut were not to be touched, except that Malemort had permission to fell beech trees to make shafts for the quarrels. No specific references to the supply of feathers have been located – quarrels could have been fletched (or winged) with thin strips of wood, horn or leather instead of swan or goose feathers.

Sometimes it is not only possible to trace a delivery of quarrels but also the use to which they were put. At the siege of Bedford Castle in 1224, 15,000 quarrels were used. These had been sent from Corfe Castle, and an order of October 1223 required 15,000 quarrels to be sent from St Briavels Castle to Corfe Castle, where they were receipted in March 1224. Unfortunately only one small arrowhead has been recovered from restricted excavations at Bedford Castle.

The Three Castles: White Castle, Skenfrith Castle and Grosmont Castle feature in many orders. 10,000 quarrels were sent to White Castle on 31 August 1233; in 1244 another 6900 were sent to John of Monmouth for delivery to the Three Castles; Gilbert Talbot was in control of the Three Castles in 1254, and another order required 6000 quarrels to be delivered to him. There was a charge of 5s for carrying quarrels from St Briavels to White Castle in 1256-7, and in 1257, the constable of Abergavenny Castle received 20 barrels of quarrels from the constable of St Briavels, and noted that seven barrels were to go on to White Castle.

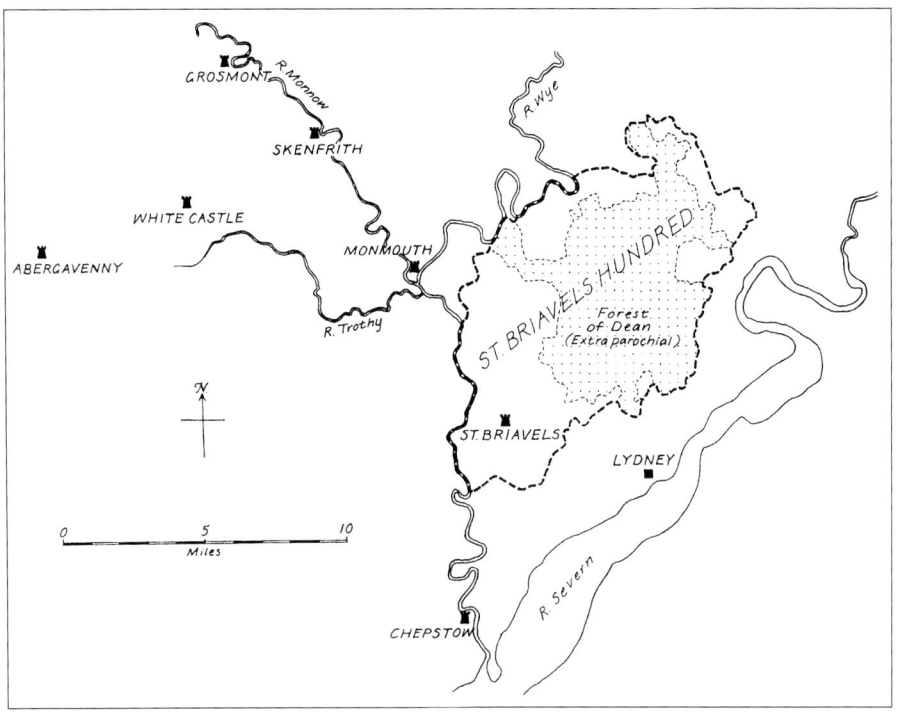

*26* Map of St Briavels and the Three Castles

Bristol was also being used as a depot for the receipt of quarrels from St Briavels Castle. It is quite likely they were carried down river to Chepstow in flat-bottomed boats called 'trows', and embarked there on ships to Bristol. There is a record of one Rogerus the Trowman to receive a grant of 2s for courageous acts at the weir – could this have been at Bigsweir where the quarrels left St Briavels?

Similar quantities were involved – 1000 to Bristol in 1233, another 1000 in 1241 and in 1244, 2000 to Bristol for trans-shipment to Richard de Clifford, constable of Lundy. Thirty thousand quarrels and bolts were to be sent without delay to Bristol in 1253. Bristol was certainly shipping quarrels out – a record in November 1284 has 10,000 quarrels for one-foot crossbows and 10,000 quarrels for two-foot crossbows being sent from St Briavels Castle to Bristol for trans-shipment to Carnarfon.

Another record reads:

> To Peter de la Mare, constable of Bristol Castle: Order to cause to be provided 400 staves *(baculos)* of Spanish yew to make crossbows, 400 nuts, 400 keys, 400 stirrups, 100 baldricks, 20 pieces of whalebone, 1000 bow strings, 100,000 quarrels for two feet, and 100,000 quarrels for one foot, and cause them to be carried to Kaernarvon, there to be delivered to Master Richard de Abindon, the King's Chamberlain there.

The figures in this translation are somewhat suspect. They are abbreviated in the original document and could as easily be read 'a hundred hundred' or 10,000.

In no case is there any indication that anything other than quarrels were supplied by St Briavels Castle. Both records date from shortly after the commencement of the building of Caernarfon Castle in June 1282. What is evident is that far more new equipment and weaponry than was immediately required was being taken into stock at the king's new castles. In the Calendar of *Welsh Rolls* of 21 October 1284 we have:

> The king has committed to John de Havering during the king's pleasure, his castle of Caernarfon, with the armour and all things forming the munition of the castle, and has granted him 200 marks yearly for the custody, to be received by the hands of the Chamberlain, on condition that he shall have continuously in garrison there, in addition to himself and his household at his cost, 40 fencible men of whom 15 shall be crossbowmen, one artiller,

a carpenter, a mason and a smith, and of the others shall be made janitors, watchmen and other necessary ministers in the castle.

The total number of quarrels made by John Malemort in those years from 1228 to 1293 could well be over a million. Possibly the greatest number were made in 1277 when the constable was ordered to have made with 'all speed', 150,000 quarrels for one-foot crossbows and 50,000 for those of two-foot 'as the king wills that quarrels shall be made and kept there for his own use'.

It is possible that John Malemort was not working alone – an Adam Malemort appears in an eyre-roll of 1258, and a Stephen Malemort held a licence for a forge in the Forest in 1282. In 1283, 170,000 quarrels are accounted for as issue to both English and Gascon crossbowmen in the Anglesey division of the army. Of these, 70,000 were brought into the country by the Gascons, the other 100,000 supplied by St Briavels.

On 8 August 1241 the constable of St Briavels Castle was ordered to facilitate the manufacture of 2000 quarrels of each of the six patterns delivered by Paul Peyvre to John Malemort, and 10,000 'fit for a crossbow to be strung with the foot' to be sent to the king at Shrewsbury. In March 1242, 50,000 thin quarrels of those in his keeping were to be sent to equip Windsor Castle, 50,000 thick to the Tower of London to equip Dover Castle and 2000 thick and 50,000 thin to Portsmouth.

The above entry for '2000 quarrels of each of six patterns' attracted the attention of Alf Webb, now President of the Dean Archaeological Group, some 40 years ago. Since then he has patiently identified the six patterns by checking deliveries to castles and examining finds made at those castles by archaeologists.

The manufacture of quarrels would not have been done within St Briavels Castle as the noise and smoke would have been unbearable. Searches have identified 'Quarrel Fields' about three quarters of a mile (1.2km) south-south-west of the castle, on a south-westerly-facing slope, with a freely-running spring water source. There was a large spread of iron slag and samples taken produced a wide variation of iron content, sufficient proof that iron was being both wrought and worked into articles.

It was becoming common for landowners to claim the ore from their lands and in 1282 the king put forward some claims of his own. In the bailiwicks of Bearse and Mitcheldean the sum of one penny per week, and in Stanton one halfpenny per week, was paid for every workman

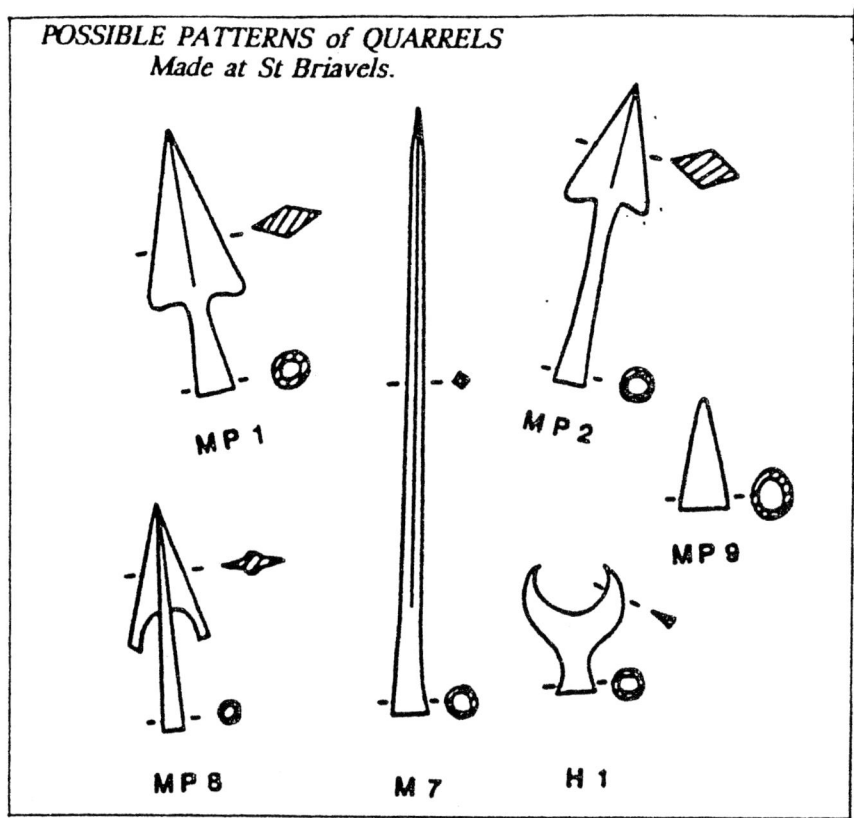

*27* The six quarrel patterns identified by Alf Webb

taking three bushels of ore and over (one bushel would equal about 8 imperial gallons or 36l). The right was also established to have one man working in each mine for 2d per day and the receipt of his own share of ore. In Abenhall and Mitcheldean the king claimed six bushels of ore per week on payment of 6d, in Bearse 24 bushels for 2s and in Staunton ore for his itinerant forge at one penny per bushel. He also claimed one halfpenny for every bushel taken from the Forest. It is known that, in the same year, Ralph of Abenhall laid claim to all ore in Abenhall, although the outcome of this claim against that of the king is not known.

In 1282 there were some 60 forges working, 5 in Littledean, 3 in Blakeney, 2 at Lydney, 13 at St Briavels, 10 at Staunton, 2 at Bicknor, 2 at Hope Mansell, 8 at Ruardean and 14 at Mitcheldean, their values ranging between 18 marks and £50.

Ralph de Sandwico, of the castle and manor of St Briavels, reported that, in 1276, he had been paid £23, 16s 9.5d from great and little mines of iron and coal, £11 and 16s from rent of forges and £5 and 15s for the sale of cinders. The methods of smelting left cinders containing appreciable amounts of iron which was of value.

King Edward I (1272-1307) demanded an annual supply of 360 bars of iron and 100 iron rods, the latter for making into nails for the fleet. The demands for iron products for warfare and like activities did not diminish. In 1333 Robert de Sapy was ordered to buy 500 pieces of iron and 5000 horseshoes, and to send them to Ireland, via Bristol, to King Edward III. Neither were the clergy timid in making demands, for on the completion of Newland church, the Bishop of Llandaff obtained from Edward III, in 1341, a grant of one tenth of the ore raised in the neighbourhood. This grant, together with the product of the Forest forges, yielded £34 in the same year.

In 1375 a familiar type of industrial dispute arose regarding demarcation lines between the activities of the iron miners, quarrymen and coal miners. It is understood that the records of King Edward III show that a Commission had to consider the matter. The Commission came to the conclusion that the 'Laws and Privileges' applied to the iron ore miners and the sea coal miners but not to the quarrymen. In fact, in the strongest possible terms, it was put that quarrymen had no rights and were not to quote the 'Laws and Privileges' of the miners and act as if they related to them!

There is then a pause in the records of ironworking activities in the Forest with only a few isolated items coming to hand. However, despite the problems the thirteenth and fourteenth centuries were very active ones for the iron industry and it was the main occupation for many during these periods. Subsequently forges had to be destroyed to protect the Forest's timber resources, a recurring problem, which were under threat due to a lack of planning.

# 5

# THE *BOOK OF DENNIS* (DEAN)

There is no doubt that Forest of Dean miners, the free miners, had a number of privileges and their own set of laws, but who granted them is subject to much debate. The title *Book of Dennis* doesn't appear until 1840 when David Mushet referred to 'an old book called Dennis'. It was supposed to be a reprint of 'The Miners Customs in the Forest of Dean'. Hart, (1953, *The Free Miners*) states that the oldest extant document containing 'The Dean Miners Laws and Privileges' is a transcript dated 16 April 1610, and is held by the Public Record Office.

On the other hand, Nicholls (1866, *Iron Making in Olden Times*) states that the first printing and publication took place in 1687, being taken from an original parchment roll transcribed by the then Gaveller, Richard Morse, in 1673. It was printed by William Cooper, at the Pelican, in Little Britain, and he claimed he had produced a true copy of this ancient and curious document, but he added 'III' after the words, 'in tyme of the Excellent and Redoubted Prince King Edward'. Tradition in the Forest certainly holds that confirmation of these customary privileges was granted by Edward I, II or III, for their very useful services in war, but no records of charters or grants have been found. Other counties have special miners' privileges – those of Cornwall were embodied in a charter of 1201 under Henry III and those of Derbyshire in Henry V's reign.

An excuse could be made that the Forest of Dean miners were not a 'corporate body' but this did not seem to stop charters being granted elsewhere. Nicholls makes the suggestion that it was probable that the Forest miners applied for, and obtained confirmation of, their privileges from William the Conqueror sometime between 1066 and 1069 – with the supply of 36 dicres of iron and 100 bars of iron to Gloucester, as recorded in *Domesday Book*, being the reason for the grant. A further uncertainty is a statement made in 1625 by a Christopher Tucker of Littledean, that he had seen 'an ancient deed dating in the reign of King Edward II testifying the liberty and privileges of the miners within the Forest'.

Perhaps the most relevant dating claim is contained in a note in Hart (1953), note 2, page 19:

> The area of which the rights were exercised seems to be that defined by the perambulations of 1228 and 1282, which rules out the reign of Edward II (1307-27) and Edward III (1327-37) seeing that in these two reigns the forest was defined by the reduced area given in the perambulations of 1300.

More relevant is what these laws and privileges allow. Briefly these are: (i) freedom to mine in any soil. subject to dues to the king and lord of the soil, (ii) free access to the mine, (iii) provision of timber for the works, (iv) the right to try all mining cases in their own court, and (v) the exclusion of all foreigners i.e. those coming from outside the area. These rights are better seen in documents of Charles II, (1675):

> Is there not and hath there not always, time whereof the memory of man is not to the contrary, been this custom there used: That any man born within that part of the hundred of the Castle of St Briavels as lyeth within the perambulation of the Forest of Dean and bred and brought up in the mystery or craft of mining, after he hath wrought in his own proper person one whole year and a day in some mine within the Forest, is and hath always been accompted and taken for a free miner, and might lawfully and hath been accustomed at his will and liking, by himself or other partners being also free miners, to enter into any place, as well as the king's waste soil or ground of the Forest, as of the several lands of any of his subjects or tenants within the Forest (except gardens, orchards and curtilages) there to dig for the finding of minerals of iron and coal, and the same so found to cast up, take, carry away and convert to his or their own proper use? (Exch.Deps.Comms 27. Chas II 1675. Interr.No.VI.)

A further note in Hart states: 'the body of free miners are referred to at various times as either "The King's Miners", "The Company of Miners", "Pyoneers" or "The Fellowship of Miners". Certain individuals within the miners were referred to as 'Master-miners'. The miners were first referred to by statute as 'Free Miners' in an Act of 1831. This was the Dean Forest Commission Act. 1831 (1 and 2 Will.IV.c 12):

> An Act for ascertaining the Boundaries of the Forest of Dean, and for inquiring into the Rights and Privileges claimed by Free Miners of the Hundred of Saint Briavel's, and for other purposes. (2nd August, 1831)

The Dean Forest Commissioners were asked to examine the matters raised by the 1831 Act and report, as necessary, to 'the Lord High Treasurer, or Lords Commissioners of his majesty's treasury'. The fourth report of the Commissioners contains several items of particular interest:

> The origin of the rights and privileges of the free miners is involved in obscurity, and we cannot upon search find anything which enables us to refer to it with certainty.
>
> The respective periods of a year and a day and of seven years as connected with the means of becoming free by working and by apprenticeship are well known in English Law, and both periods are in operation for this purpose among the free miners, a year and a day being the time required for working in the case of a person born in the hundred of a parent, and seven years for the apprenticeship of the son of a person not free.
>
> To whatever circumstances the origin may be referred, it seems to be a reasonable foundation for it that the reserving a certain share of the produce to the landlord, and giving up the remainder as the price of the labour of getting it, would be a convenient mode of having the mines worked. This appears to have prevailed also in the mines of Cornwall, Mendipp, and Derbyshire, and is now very usual in working mines.
>
> Traces of the existence of the Forest of Dean miners are certainly to be found in early history. It appears that they were summoned to attend the royal armies in the reigns of Edward I and II and there is a tradition in the forest that exclusive privileges were given to them in consequence of their services at the siege of Berwick.

Also of interest is the information from the *Rotuli Scotiae*, Vol. 1, p91:

> Writ, dated 2 August 1310, commands the constable of Saint Briavels and keeper of the Forest of Dean, to select 100 archers and 12 miners and

conduct them to Berwick-upon-Tweed. (From *The Laws of The Dean Forest and Hundred of Saint Briavels, in the County of Gloucester*, written in 1878 by James G. Wood, M.A., LL.B.)

The foregoing seems to establish the rights and privileges of the free miners and also the means whereby the son of a 'person not free' could serve an apprenticeship to become a free miner. Regarding the grant of the privileges the 'writ, dated 2 August 1310' puts that in the third year of the reign of Edward II (1307-27) and this might reasonably be seen as the time of origin of the grant.

# 6

# FIFTEENTH CENTURY TO THE CIVIL WAR

By 1435 dues were still being collected from miners and transporters of iron ore and coal, and from those taking cinders. Forges were permitted under an annual payment of 7s a forge. There were 33 forges working in 1436 – fourteen in the area of the bailiff of Great Dean, two in Little Dean, two in Ruardean, ten for a full year and one for half a year in Newland, one for half a year at Lydney and three elsewhere. In 1435-6 the king commenced farming out the proceeds of iron mines and Hugh Cromwale, on behalf of the Duke of Bedford, accounted for £22. In 1446 the Earl of Warwick paid £100 per annum as rent for the Forest, followed in 1464 by the Duke of Clarence and later by the Duke of Gloucester. The Duke of Norfolk's accounts for 1462-69 show that arrowhead makers were then paid at the rate of five for one penny. It is also worthy of note that John Lake, arrowhead maker to Henry VIII (1509-47), was paid 4d a day with food and board!

Production of iron had dropped steadily from its peak in the thirteenth century but the industry was still very important and, in 1519-20, a large number of 'smyth holders' signed an acceptance of an arbitration award regarding a dispute between the people of east Dean and west Dean which appears to have arisen from trade in the iron industry. There is no management information or details of employment and remuneration in Dean documents but an account, in 1531, of a forge worked by men from Dean for Henry VIII at Llantrisant, Glamorgan, seems to represent the local practice:

> Five men kept the fire to melt the ore, having 12d a day each after the manner of the Forest of Dean, four others worked at the bellows, where

three blow at a time and one stands void to refresh the others for he blows six or seven hours at every gadde that is melting and thus they make two gaddes a day, each weighing 1 hundredweight [50.8 kg]. Each blower was paid 7.5d a day and 12d more was paid to the four. One man hewed timber to stay the mine at 6d a day and three charcoal burners were likewise paid that wage.

Production was small for it took nine men working 12-14 hours a day to make 2 hundredweights (approximately 100kg) of iron a day.

Although the blast furnace was introduced into England in 1469, at Newbridge in Ashdown Forest, it did not reach Dean until the 1500s but its arrival heralded a substantial improvement in the production of iron. Blast furnaces could be in continuous operation for six to nine months a year requiring a substantial water supply to drive a waterwheel which operated the bellows providing the blast. This requirement alone

*28* Blacksmiths at work, woodcut published *c*.1568. *From Amman and Sacks 1973*

caused some centralisation of the industry as they moved to sites of powerful streams and waterways. The first charcoal blast furnace was set up at Whitchurch on the Forest border by Gilbert, Earl of Shrewsbury, and the second Earl of Wessex, Robert Devereux, had two furnaces at Bishopswood and a forge at Lydbrook from the early 1590s. Robert Devereux was executed in 1601 and the property, of which no record has been found of any production, was seized by the Crown. The person to whom we can most likely give the honour of the first commercial introduction of the blast furnace into the Forest of Dean is probably the constable of St Briavels in 1608 – William Herbert, Earl of Pembroke. He was also governor of the Corporation of Mineral Works drawing wire by power at Tintern, under a patent granted to William Humfrey and Christopher Shutz in 1565.

A reasonable amount is known about one of the furnaces of the time – Parkend, built in 1612. It was surveyed in 1635 and that record is still available. Around 1812 David Mushet inspected the site and supplied information to Abraham Rees who drew sketches and wrote an explanatory text. Schubert (1953) copied the drawings and added further details which are illustrated here.

*Figure* (*a*) is a cross section at the tapping aperture. The base was about 22ft square (6.7m), and walls rose vertically for 5ft (1.5m) where the hearth

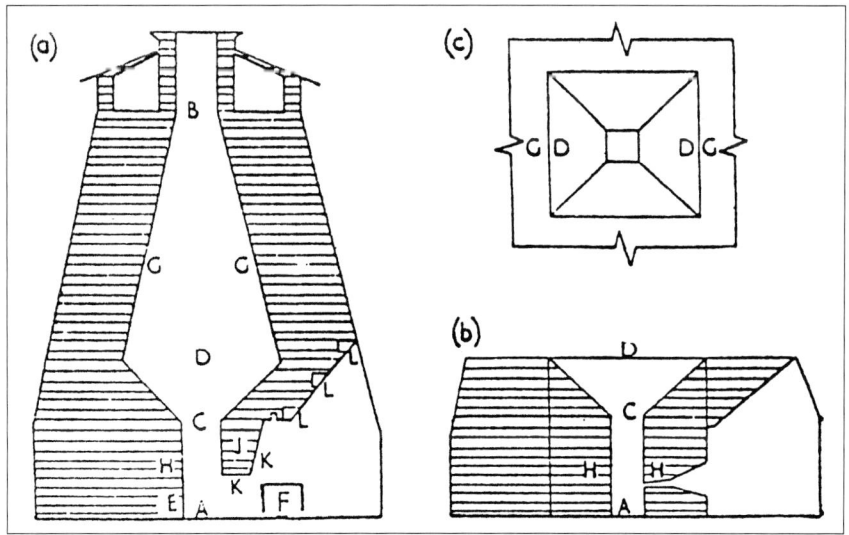

*29* Parkend Furnace

joined to boshes (C), and then the upper part continued as a form of truncated pyramid. The inner lining (G) was a 'thin bed of infusable species of sandstone' and the space between this and the outer walls was filled with sand. The hearth (H), of similar sandstone, was 4ft (1.2m) high and 4ft (1.2m) wide. Also depicted are E to F, with E being the backwall and F the dam stone. The arch was strengthened by cast iron 'sows' (L) arcing across.

At the very back of the arch was the tymp stone (J), protected underneath and outside by the tymp plate (K). A buckstave, a vertical iron plate, protected each side of the space between the tymp stone and the bottom. Another iron plate, the dam plate, covered the dam stone. This had a notch through which the slag ran. On one side of the dam stone another notch, usually closed with clay, was opened whenever molten iron was tapped, which ran into a furrow made in a bed of sand. When casting small objects, the metal was ladled into moulds.

*Figure (b)* is a cross section where the other tuyere arch was. The tuyere contained the nozzles of a pair of bellows which were operated by iron

*30* Parkend Iron Works *c.*1890

cams worked by a waterwheel of 22ft (6.7m) diameter. *Figure (c)* is a horizontal section of the furnace at the top of the boshes. There is a lot more information in the Schubert report, which is given in some detail in Hart (1971) who also gives details of the survey of 1635 when Parkend consisted of 2 hammers, 3 fineries and 1 chafery. The forge was destroyed in the Civil War in 1644 and rebuilt and reused between 1662 and 1674, finally being demolished by 1674. All these works needed a good and regular supply of water, and that requirement became the prime locational factor, making discovery much easier for the archaeologist – find the water and you find the furnace, whereas the bloomery furnaces are found usually part way up south-west-facing slopes.

An impetus to mining was given in the late sixteenth century by the establishment of blast furnaces at Whitchurch, Lydbrook and Lydney. There was great demand for ore from Ireland and, around 1613, 6000 cartloads of iron ore at 30s a load, and 6000 of cinders at 15s a load, were sent to Ireland via the Severn and the Wye. In 1666, two vessels from Pembrokeshire, laden with cinders from Dean, were taken by the French or the Dutch.

Another alteration that arose when the new charcoal blast furnaces came was the practice of 'bargains'. For instance, on 17 February 1612, William, Earl of Pembroke, made a bargain to pay '4s for 12,000 cords yearly for 21 years, or £200 per annum, with £33 6s 8d besides, all for fuel only'. He was, however:

> to have allowance of reasonable fireboote for the workmen out of the dead and dry wood, and to inclose a garden not exceeding half an acre to every house, and likewise to inclose for the neccessity of the works the number of 12 acres [4.8ha] to every several works; the houses and enclosures to be pulled down and laid open as the works shall cease or remove.

Similar bargains were made in 1615, by a Sir Basil Brook and Robert Chaldecott. Nicholls (1866) gives details on a number of them.

Wood for charcoal was abundant. Very many areas have been located where the charcoal clamps have been burnt and there are large numbers of complaints recorded of charcoal burners felling trees rather than using fallen timber. Coppices and underwood were best for charcoal and there were restrictions on felling oak, beech or ash, within 14 miles (22.5km)of any navigable river. It was said that it required five and a half short cords of wood to make a load of charcoal and at least two loads of charcoal were required to make 1 ton of iron. Charcoal burners could receive 45s a load for large charcoal but this price fell to half for the small pieces and dust.

The first water-powered wire mill in Britain was erected at Tintern in 1566. William Humfrey, Assay Master of the Royal Mint, obtained the capital and the new mill was intended to make Britain less dependent on imports of substantial quantities of wire. Initially it was intended to make brass and brass wire and Humfrey obtained the help of Christopher Schutz of Saxony but they soon started to draw iron wire instead. They encountered a problem with local iron which was not of the same ductility, or purity, as the Swedish 'Osmond' iron so some experts from Germany were imported who used a new method of careful decarburisation of the iron to achieve the required standard. The process for mass-production of iron wire was developed to a sequence of three operations: (i) the iron bar was 'strained', or forged, into a rod about as large as one's little finger, (ii) using water power the rod was 'ripped' to coarse wire about the size of large packing thread, and (iii) the iron was annealed to soften it before it was drawn by hand into fine wire.

Eventually iron wire drawing proved lucrative and much was produced and sold. In 1568 the works were taken over by the Company of the Mineral and Battery Works who held the lease until 1631. It was said that by 1597 there were 5000 workers employed across the country manufacturing

*31* Woodcut from Biringuccio's *Pirotechnia* (1540) showing production of coarse wire

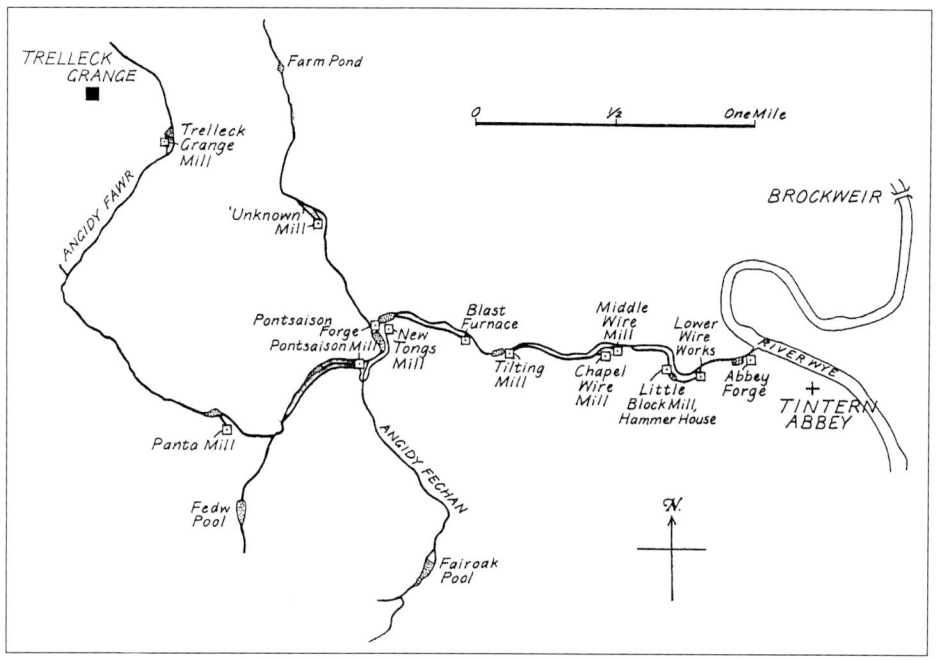

*32* Plan of industrial sites on the Angidy River system near Tintern

goods from Tintern wire. The demand for wire resulted in the Company building a second wire works in 1606-7 at Whitebrook, a few miles north of Tintern.

The 1600s were a period of confusion but the early part was a great industrial time; for example, in 1612-3 some 1400 tons of iron ore was sent to Ireland alone. Later, disputes arose between the ironmasters and the miners and the disputes, together with the illegal taking of trees, led the Crown to suspend ironworking in 1613 but it commenced again when works were re-let in 1615. The ironmasters continued the illegal felling of timber and the Crown again suspended ironworking in 1617.

In 1621 the king's iron works were leased for seven years to Richard Challoner and Philip Harris and timbers assigned for their repair. The Crown appointed 'overseers' to regulate the taking of timber. For some years the industry flourished but in 1625 the lessees were accused of the misappropriation of timber. They were working a furnace and double forge at Parkend, a furnace and forge at Lydbrook together with another rented from George Vaughan of nearby Courtfield. All were in regular use but a furnace at Cannop and a furnace and forge at Soudley were not. The Crown decided to let the lease run to its due end in 1628 but a struggle for concessions ensued in 1627. The applicants were Sir Sackville Crowe of Laughern in Carmarthenshire, late treasurer of the Navy, Sir John Kyrle, ironmaster in Herefordshire and Brooke with George Mynne and Thomas Hackett of the wire works at Tintern and Whitebrook of the Company of the Mineral and Battery Works. The Earl of Pembroke, one of the governors of the Company, obtained the concession in December 1627 for 21 years and sub-let to Brooke, Mynne and Hackett. The lease ran until 1633 by which time the Crown was being urged to suppress the others and run its own iron works. Once again there were claims of the disastrous effect on the woodlands.

In 1634 a list of iron works in or near Dean was assembled. The Crown owned four furnaces and five forges and private operators owned seven furnaces and six forges. Sir John Winter owned two forges, Lydbrook Middle Forge was owned by Vaughan and a small forge in Coleford by Anthony Hamon. Winter's furnace at Rodmore had been established in 1629 by John Powell of Preston, Herefordshire, and Kyrle probably owned a furnace at Bishopswood.

Sir John Winter enjoyed a favoured position in being the private secretary to Queen Henrietta Maria, wife of Charles I, and was eventually treated favourably by an important Forest Court for Dean, held in 1634, which halted all negotiations and put leases in abeyance. The court dealt with some 800 offences of which 420 related to misappropriation of trees and some with unauthorised building of iron works. Ultimately applications by Sir Baynham Throckmorton, of Clearwell, and Sir Sackville Crowe, with others, were successful. However, there was intrigue at Court and Winter, pardoned for his misdemeanours by the 1634 court, was granted, in March 1640, 'all His Majesty's lands waste, soil, minerals, and trees and underwood in Dean' comprising 17-18,000 acres (about 7200ha). It was virtually a sale of that area of Dean Forest for around £106,000! Admittedly, Lea Bailey, Chestnut Wood and the woods of Kidnalls were excluded as was 15,000 tons (15,240 tonnes) of ships timber. He also had to permit Throckmorton and his partners to work the furnaces at Soudley and Parkend and the forges at Soudley, Parkend, Whitecroft and Bradley, and allow them to take 13,500 cords of wood yearly, but he owned the furnaces and forges at Lydney, Lydbrook, Cannop, Rodmore and Gunns Mill. Great numbers of trees and whole areas of underwood were being felled by Winter, and he had enclosed 4000 acres (1618.4ha) to allow regrowth.

The local inhabitants strongly disapproved of Winter's actions and, in June 1640, they partitioned the Crown that their rights should be respected. Some protracted litigation resulted in the House of Commons voting for termination of Winter's grant in March 1642. To pay Winter's debts the iron works were leased to Thomas Morgan. The timber that Winter had felled was sold, some to John Browne, the king's gun founder. Browne did not operate any of the works in the forest but assigned them to nominees. Cannop and Lydbrook went to Donning, Bradley to Tipper and Throckmorton had others.

There are several oblique references to the manufacture of guns in the forest and particularly at Gunns Mill, but none appear to have supporting evidence. Despite that it is a reasonable presumption that both guns and cannon balls were manufactured in the forest although some of the precise sites may not be identified. It has been recorded that 610 guns were ordered by the Crown on behalf of the States General of Holland in 1629 and the place of manufacture was presumed to be Gunns Mill, and H.G. Nicholls stated that 'an ancient piece of ordnance' was found there and 'Guns Pill' was the place where they were afterwards shipped. It has been held that the statement regarding the manufacture cannot be verified and Guns Pill has not yet been identified on the Severn. Nevertheless, it is probably reasonable to support the view that the presumption is correct.

We do know that Sir Sackville Crowe, a known active gun-founder, moved out of the Sussex Weald around 1634-6, possibly due to the shortage of wood for the furnaces. The State Papers for 1634 include details of Crowe's tender for the manufacture of iron guns in the Forest of Dean. He was probably keen to enter the market because the European demand for guns was high due to the Thirty Years' War which involved most of western Europe between 1618 and 1648. Crowe's tender won the work on July 12 1636 and he was given a 21-year lease to manufacture iron guns in the forest. He had three partners: Sir Baynham Throckmorton of Clearwell and two Bristol merchantmen, John Taylor and John Gonning. Under this partnership the king's iron works at Lydbrook, Soudley and Parkend were revitalised and expanded and Dr Hart has commented that 'a concentration of such large iron works was probably, at this time, unique in England'. The partnership lasted four years until, in 1640, their lease was brutally revised by the Crown when John Winter was given control of the king's iron works from 1 April, 1640.

King Charles raised his standard at Nottingham on 22 August 1642 to signify that he was at war with the Commons, and so the troubles of the Civil War 'in which the country surrounding the Forest was so much involved' disturbed iron manufacture. During the Civil War iron furnaces and forges changed hands with the flow of Royalist and Parliamentary control. The iron works at Lydney, Parkend, Cannop and Whitecroft were partially destroyed, and what was left leased to Winter's opponent, Massey, in 1644. Massey assigned Captain Gifford to the furnace and two forges at Lydney and the Park (Upper) Furnace. Kyrle had the Bishopwood Furnace and Brayne, in partnership with Kyrle, had the furnace at Redbrook and Rodmore, and a forge was built at Rodmore. In 1644 Brayne seized the Cannop and Lydbrook works from Donning.

By 1645 Brayne was also working Gunns Mill, Bradley and Lydbrook's second forge near Howbrook. In October 1646, Brayne was ordered to deliver up the Redbrook Furnace and, by June the following year, Massey sold any further interest in the ironworking under a five-year lease for £2000. Thomas Morgan and his partners fought to undo this, claiming their lease from Winter should still stand.

The record of the individual furnaces and forges show this to-and-fro pattern during the Civil War. Parkend was built in 1612, repaired 1631 and destroyed in 1644. Cannop was built in 1612, worked intermittently from 1621 to 1625, rebuilt in 1626 and destroyed in 1644. At Lydbrook there were two privately owned forges built in the early 1590s, and another built in 1610 – these were known as Upper, Middle and Lower Forges. In 1612 another was built at Howbrook, which worked intermittently from 1613 to 1625, and was rebuilt in 1632. It was leased to Throckmorton in 1636 and handed over to the Donnings in 1642, seized by Brayne in 1644 and partly destroyed in 1650 by the Preservators of the Forest. Upper Forge, Lydbrook, had disappeared by 1668 and Middle Forge became known as Upper Forge. Both Upper and Lower Forges remained in occasional use.

A private forge was built at Whitecroft in 1628-9 and destroyed in 1644; a new one built on, or near, the site in 1654 remained in use until 1661 and was demolished in 1674 when part became a corn mill. Soudley Furnace was built in 1612, run by Skinner, taken over by Brayne in 1644 and destroyed in 1650. King's Forge, probably on the present site of the Dean Heritage Museum, was built in 1612, destroyed in 1644 and sold for demolition in 1674. The wheelpit has been excavated by the Dean Heritage.

In 1634 there were two single furnaces at Flaxley run by Tipper but owned by Sir John Winter who held the woods at Flaxley. Gunns Mill was built in

*33* A mortar of the type used against Goodrich Castle

1628 and owned by Winter, but it was taken in 1644 and run by Brayne. It was probably fully destroyed by 1650. At Longhope it seems that a furnace called 'Hope' was built around 1656 and ran until 1680. The site has not yet been fully located but it was probably built near the Church Farm. There is no evidence of a furnace here either before or during the Civil War.

Brockweir or Bigsweir is perhaps mentioned in a document of 1634 but is given as Brickweare so it could refer to either. Attempts have been made to locate it but it is thought probable that it refers to an earlier works at Coed Ithel on the opposite side of the River Wye. A furnace was built at Rodmore by 1629, run by Sir John Winter in 1634 but seized by Kyrle in 1645; it probably went out of use by 1680 after which it became a forge and later a corn mill. Near Rodmore, shown as Rowley, but possibly known as Atkin's or Burnt Mill, another furnace was run by Brayne and Kyrle.

Sir Edward Winter built a furnace in 1604 a little to the north of his house, White Cross, and a forge to the south-east which later became known as Lower Forge. By 1607 he had Upper Forge running on the Newerne Brook, later to become known as Middle Forge. In 1644 all were partially destroyed by Massey, who then had them repaired and leased to Gifford. By 1653 they were run for the Commonwealth until finally restored to the Winter family in 1660.

Two furnaces operated at Bishopwood, one possibly built in early 1588. They became Benedict Hall's property in 1633 with Kyrle as tenant. He lost them during the Civil War and they were demolished by order of the Preservators of the Forest in 1650. Redbrook had two furnaces, one built *c*.1604 and shown on the '1608' map; the other was built close to that date but not shown on the map. Both furnaces were seized in 1645 and run by Kyrle and Brayne.

The Civil War greatly affected all the iron manufacturing in Dean with many furnaces and forges destroyed or made temporarily useless. Probably those that remained in operation were used to produce cannon balls and mortar shells rather than any other iron use. There is no record of any iron making from 1650 until mid-1653 and it was not until September 1653 that full debtor and creditor accounts were commenced. It is significant that from September 1653 until August 1655, iron making in the Forest cost £12,607 16s, but income was only £10,705 14s. Perhaps this should have been an indication that the state could not run such businesses.

Once the Commonwealth ceased and Charles II regained the throne, a number of petitions were brought seeking to return the iron making to private hands. In the Forest of Dean there were numerous claimants. Sir Hugh Middleton was one who claimed that Major John Wade was:

> put in by Cromwell and that Wade, in July last [1659], robbed him of horses and arms and kept him in close imprisonment for supporting his Majesty, and has several times ransacked his house.

From a different quarter was an application from Massey, who stated that he had formerly held the works, but everything had been taken from him by the 'Rump Parliament' for his loyalty. Sir John Winter was a third and probably reasonable applicant, saying yea before all the troubles that had consumed this kingdom, he was the true owner of all these works.

Sir Baynham Throckmorton also unsuccessfully claimed, although he had a number of works which he was expressly allowed to continue using when Sir John Winter was granted the rest of the Forest's iron works.

Sir John Winter's claim was the one accepted. The grant supporting the claim was most comprehensive and gave Winter all the timber in the Forest except that fit for shipbuilding, bestowed on him the power to execute the Forest Laws on all offenders and to receive for himself all fines arising from the Forest Courts. He was to make parishes, create and endow churches, to grant exemption from any public service to his tenants and servants, to have all royalties and privileges, and fisheries in the River Severn. He was granted the right to all royal mines and treasure trove, and he had the power to cut down all trees, saplings and underwood and to convert the land to any use he pleased – notwithstanding the provision of former Acts.

It is hardly surprising that, once again, his operations caused discontent among the local people, and after much protesting, the Commons appointed a Committee of Enquiry. This Committee made a new agreement with Winter in which he surrendered his original grant in exchange for £30,000 and all the timber not fit for the Navy, together with the use of the king's iron works, mines and cinders, reserving for his use the woods of Kidnalls. In a separate bargain he obtained 20,000 cords of wood blown down in Lea Bailey.

Less than a year later alarm was again raised concerning the quantity of timber that Winter was cutting in the Forest and an attempt was made to pass a bill in Parliament to preserve the woods and timbers of the forest. Finally the Dean Forest [Reafforestation] Act became law. At the same time the forge at Whitecroft and two furnaces at Parkend and Howbrook were denied Dean cordwood, and the works at Parkend were sold to Paul Foley for demolition. So ended 64 years of the king's iron works, the administration of which had fluctuated between the needs of the Navy and the demands of the Exchequer. Winter, possibly through Court influence, retained his right to timber granted to him in 1662, except for ship timber. A Committee of Peers reported back that they considered Winter to be entitled to some compensation, and as he was a debtor to the king of a sum of £6690, they requested the king to remit that debt and allow Winter to have the return of all seized timber. The king agreed. In Winter's defence it must be stated that, although he had been frequently accused of not supplying sufficient timber to the Navy, yet in 1662 the Navy itself stated that there was no timber fit for its use anywhere in the 18,000 acres (7283ha) granted to Winter.

The Dean Forest [Reafforestation] Act 1668, was designed to:

> restore and preserve the growth of timber for the future supply of his majesty's Royal Navy, and the maintenance of shipping for the trade of this nation.

The Act required the enclosure of 10,000 acres of the Forest of Dean, probably in 1000-acre parcels. Commissioners could sell decayed trees and those which would not form timber to help with the cost of enclosures. All work had to be completed within two years, and when enclosures were subsequently opened an equal area would be enclosed. Penalties were imposed for unlawful felling. The king could restore deer but not in excess of 800 head. Pannage could be restored after Michaelmas 1687 and, in general, privileges were safeguarded (from James G. Wood, M.A., LL.B.).

Much iron was shipped to Ireland via the Wye and Severn during the late seventeenth century. The Free Miners had their own Mine Law Court and, in 1674, made regulations concerning the loading and carrying of ore. It was agreed that the future measures of ore should be according to the 'Winchester bushel', where three bushels made a barrow. In 1677 Yarranton wrote of:

> great number of men, horses and carriages, of digging the great and infinite quantities of cinders in vast mounts above and below ground, which make the prime and best iron.

Ore continued to be shipped to Ireland from Cone Pill on the Severn and Brockwier on the Wye although prices for this trade were relatively low.

# 7

# THE SEVENTEENTH AND EIGHTEENTH CENTURIES

In 1672 Paul Foley of Stoke Edith, Herefordshire, purchased the 'whole of the materials of the king's works' in the Forest of Dean, and that was the beginning of a 75-year involvement in the iron industry of the Forest. In 1674 Paul Foley admitted his brother Philip to a one-third share in his furnaces at Longhope, Bishopswood, Redbrook and Flaxley, and to his two forges at Lydbrook and two at Flaxley.

There were many old and decayed trees, areas of coppice and underwood available for producing charcoal. Experiments in the use of Dean coal had been unsuccessful and charcoal remained the most suitable fuel for smelting. There was increased activity in iron works at Lydney, Rodmore, Rowley, Barnedge, Redbrook, Lydbrook, Bishopswood, Flaxley, Soudley, Longhope, Blakeney and the rebuilt Gunns Mill. On the periphery of the Forest area works at Tintern, Whitchurch, St Weonards, Elmbridge and Linton received ore and cinders from Dean.

In the previous chapter we referred to the fact that the site of a furnace at Longhope could not be identified, but records show that it was standing in 1680 and that a new lease of it was made to Paul Foley from Nourse Yate of Painswick on 27 June, 1682, for 15 years at £60 a year. Foley was required to carry out repairs to the premises. In 1682 a traveller left an interesting account of the works:

> From Ross we went to Longhope, and turning a little out of the road saw the furnace or kiln where they melt iron. The bellows, being very great, which gave furious blasts to the fire, are driven like an overshot mill with water,

having a great wheel divers yards in diameter. The fire to melt the ore in the furnace made of stone, which may be 7 or 8yds from bottom to top in height, is made of charcoal, burning day and night for some months, viz: so long as the water, which is but a small stream, and commonly dry in summer, doth last. The flame mounts fiercely a good height above the furnace. Here is also at the bottom of the furnace a hole as big as that of an oven which lets the dross run away in fiery streaming flames from the melted metal or ore, which metal once in 4 hours is let run into bars or other forms of iron, but the dross when cold becomes a green glassy stone, of which they have vast mounds or heaps about the house, and good for nothing but to mend the highway; the heap of charcoal was also great, and the men work day and night in their turns.

The Crown was urged by Commissioners to build a furnace and two forges to utilise the abundance of cordwood to produce bar-iron, shot and guns for the Navy, and show an appreciable saving over the ready money it paid to others to make these items for them. However, the Crown decided to sell the cordwood to iron works in Herefordshire and Monmouthshire. In 1692 a contract was made with John Wheeler and Richard Avenant, of the Foley partnership, for 60,000 short cords of 'two foot wood' which raised £20,000 for the Crown over seven years. (See also appendix 7: *Account 1*.)

There was a great deal of Forest pig iron exported to the Birmingham area due to the natural toughness of that material. Coal measures ironstones were of a much poorer 'coldshort' quality due largely to the higher proportion of phosphorus in these ores. Birmingham and the central Shropshire regions were practically self-sufficient in 'coldshort' pig but they were unable to make the tough pig required both for refining into merchant bar, for the best wrought ironwork, and for blending with 'coldshort' pig in the refinery to make bar of intermediate and lower quality for nailers and other trades requiring that material.

Records show that the Tintern Furnace, in 1672-3, yielded 1142 tons (1160 tonnes) in a 'burn' over 62 weeks, and in 1675-6 a 'blow' of 61 weeks produced 1034 tons (1050 tonnes). So that particular furnace was a very efficient one for its time and depended for its iron on a mixed charge of cinders and ore in the ratio of 2:1. The ore came in part from the Forest and in part from a source local to Tintern. The two Tintern Forges were the principal users of the iron but large amounts went to local forge masters, like Sir Robert Clayton, and greater amounts, thanks to the tidewater situation at Tintern, left the Forest by boat for South Wales and the Midlands.

In April 1680 the Mine Laws Court issued an 'Order' fixing the prices at which 12 Winchester bushels of iron mine should be delivered to various furnaces. Most localities had elements remaining from a long tradition of iron manufacture, especially St Weonards, Whitchurch, Bishopswood and Flaxley where the 'energetic proprietress', Mrs Boevey, is said to have had (*c*.AD 1712) 'a furnace for casting of iron and three forges'. Charcoal is the only fuel of which any indication remains with the coppice woods, from which the charcoal was made, being preserved. Additionally, the furnaces are shown to have been invariably situated where water power was available.

Three furnaces in blast in 1692 were Blakeney, Bishopswood and Elmbridge (Oxenhall). Blakeney was an efficient furnace producing an average of 20 tons (20.32 tonnes) of iron a week while in blast, and Bishopswood differed only in sending its product to the river port of Newnham for carriage to the Midland market. The River Wye was not particularly effective as a transport medium above the tidal limit at Brockweir. It was used between Redbrook and Brockweir and on the lower tidal reaches, but it was said to be some three times more expensive to use than the Severn. For some of the time Elmbridge (Oxenhall) drew its ore from the Forest and cinders from Cannop and Mitcheldean, but it also used a coal measure ironstone so its metallurgical performance is unclear.

In 1716-7 Redbrook Furnace produced a small quantity of coke-smelted iron, the coke being 'charked' coal, but the value of the metal produced was not as good quality as the charcoal-melted iron so it did not appeal to masters used to tough Forest pig iron. The scheme was not repeated.

Reference to the list of furnaces and forges in the '1717 List' can give an interesting indication of the large share of pig iron production which was in the hands of the Foleys between 1707-12. The production capacity of the region was 4950 tons (5029 tonnes) and Foley's production was 3500 tons (3556 tonnes). At that time the Forest forges could utilise 2300 tons (2337 tonnes) of pig iron leaving a surplus of 2650 tons (2692 tonnes), most of which went to the Birmingham–Stour Valley region and Central Shropshire. In the other direction forges in Tredegar, Carmarthen and Pembrokeshire were regularly supplied with pig iron.

The significance of the Forest of Dean in the iron industry of England and Wales and the extent of the Foley interests in the Forest, relative to

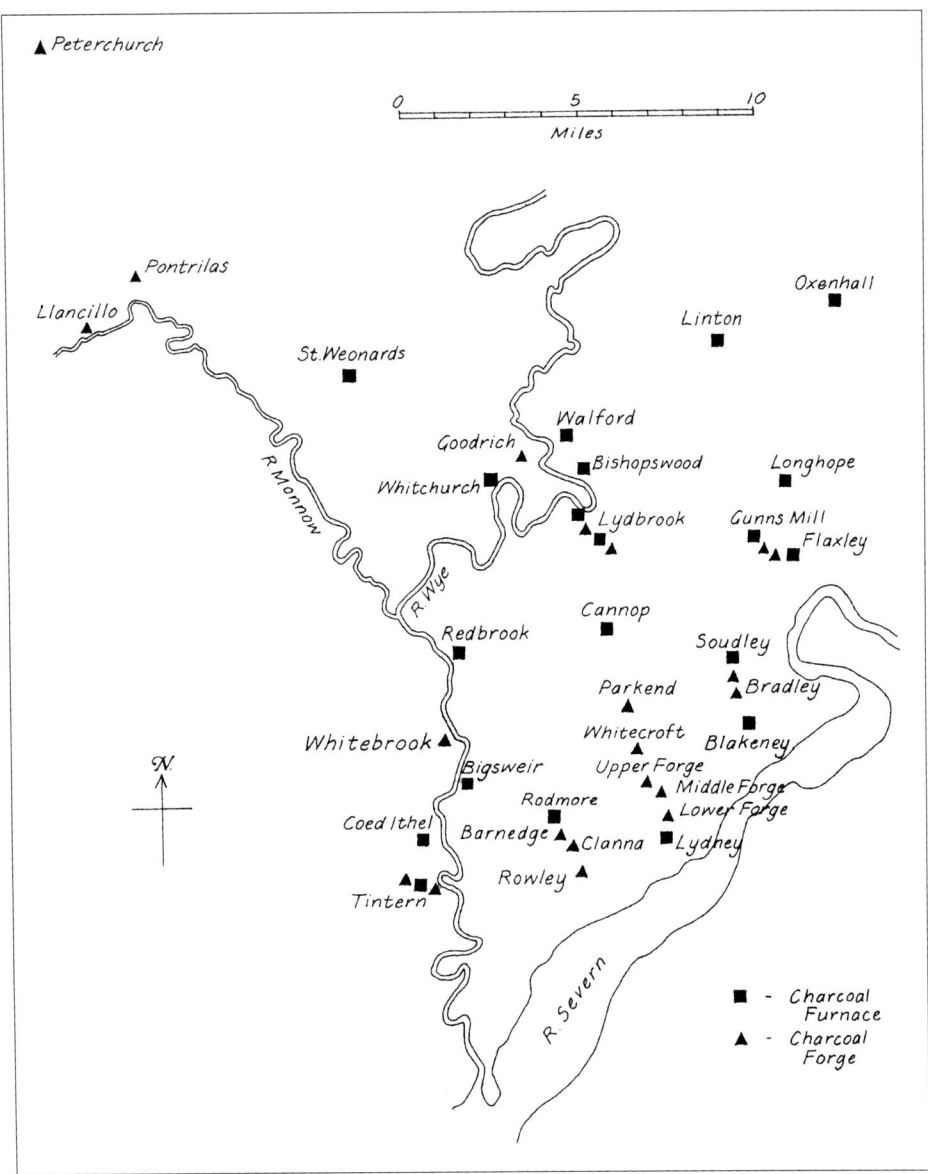

*34* Map of charcoal blast furnaces and forges in Dean and its vicinity during the seventeenth and eighteenth centuries

other ironmasters, is explained in the early list of furnaces and forges, called the '1717 List' published by E.W. Hulme, and titled *The Statistical History of the British Iron Trade from 1717 to 1750*. The yearly output of furnaces and forges in England and Wales between 1717 and 1750 in tons (tonnes) is as follows:

| Furnaces | | Forges | |
|---|---|---|---|
| Lydney | 250 (254) | Lydney x 2 | 150 (152.4) |
| Blakeney | 600 (609.6) | Blakeney | 80 (81.28) |
| Redbrook | 600 (609.6) | Lydbrook x 2 | 160 (162.56) |
| Gunns Mill | 200 (203.2) | Rowley | 40 (40.64) |
| Flaxley | 700 (711.2) | Barnedge | 80 (81.28) |
| | | Rodmore | 20 (20.32) |
| | | Newent | 120 (121.92) |

In the detail it must be remembered that pig iron is the product of the blast furnace which is run out into moulds, generally of sand, where the main run is called a 'sow' and the right angle side runs are called 'pigs' – a derivation of a sow suckling her piglets.

St Weonards Furnace, with the three forges at Lancillo, Pontrilas and Peterchurch, operated as a separate unit. The furnace did not blow in 1677-8 but sent 956 tons (971 tonnes) of sow iron to Lancillo and Pontrilas. Peterchurch usually drew its sow from St Weonards but, in this year, their balance was sufficient to make 53 tons (53.8 tonnes) of bar-iron. Both Pontrilas and Lancillo were larger forges and produced 89 tons (99.5 tonnes) and 150 tons (152.5 tonnes) respectively. Peterchurch was more isolated and served a more local market, including Hereford, but all these works shared the facilities provided by Monmouth Storehouse. Another common feature to these works was that they, as well as others, relied on Hales Furnace in the Stour Valley for their forge hammers. Forest iron, which was tough yet pliable, was unsuitable for these hammers – which weighed 5-10 hundredweights each (127-254kg). Heavy hammers and anvils were the essential tools of all forges and an average forge would use six hammers and two anvils in a year's production.

Between 1704 and 1709 Foleys held Monmouth Forge and the Lydbrook Forge from 1708-9. The total output of these works was some 200 tons (203 tonnes) per year. The major part of that output was drawn out, in charcoal-burning hearths, of Merchant bar-iron which was sold in

Bristol and the Severn towns of Gloucester, Tewkesbury and Bewdley. The Upper Forge at Lydbrook specialised in the manufacture of Osmond iron for the wire works at Tintern and Whitebrook. Most of the finished wire went to Bristol where it was handled by Samual Wallis's storehouse which forwarded large consignments to London, by land and sea, and there were agencies at Bewdley and Gloucester for the retail of wire.

There is a gap in continuity from 1717-25 which may indicate partnership changes. In 1725 there were three forges and six furnaces under the possible 'new' partnership. Four of the furnaces Elmbridge (Oxenhall), Bishopswood, Redbrook and St Weonards were working. The general pattern of trade had not altered appreciably but certain changes were noticeable for 'Lancashire Mine' or 'Red Mine' appeared in the furnace charge at Elmbridge (Oxenhall) during 1725-29. Not only imported ore, but also imported pig iron, was appearing in some of the Forest of Dean works!

Some surface mining of ore was carried out but from around 1675 many of the 'old men's workings' were made – often limited by ground water levels. George Wyrral (1780) said 'there are, deep in the earth, vast caverns scooped out by men's hands, and large as the aisles of churches'. These caverns, or 'churns', were discovered by nineteenth-century miners and found to be enormous and at tremendous depths – at Edghill 160yds (146m) and at Clearwell Caves 181yds (166m) below ground level.

Although the Foley Partnership had almost a monopoly in Dean from 1692 to the 1750s some others did come into the industry. In 1723 Lydney Iron Works were let to John Ruston of Worcester and to others in 1733. Rowland Pytt took a lease of Lydney Furnace and forges in 1740 and of Redbrook Furnace and two forges at Lydbrook in 1742. However, Thomas Daniel and Richard Reynolds, ironmasters of Bristol, made an unsuccessful attempt to erect a new furnace at Mitcheldean in 1747. The local iron trade was good up until around 1758 but then became depressed, perhaps partly due to the 'political, taxation and war' situation around 1761, and suffered further decline into 1767. After the mid-eighteenth century cordwood was less plentiful and serious negotiations were required to secure adequate supplies. Cordwood from Lord Gage's estates around Highmeadow Woods was supplied to Redbrook Furnace and two Lydbrook forges in 1742. The lessees of Lydney Furnace and forges received cordwood from Thomas Bathurst's coppices in 1768. Bathurst also endeavoured to obtain as much cordwood as possible from Dean but he was also responsible for raising the price of cordwood. In 1781 a traveller noted that wood in Dean was still plentiful 'notwithstanding the frequency of the iron furnaces'. All the charcoal blast furnaces, except Flaxley, Lydney and Redbrook, and all the forges, except Lydney, Lydbrook and Flaxley, were closed by the end of the century. The furnace at Flaxley ran until 1802, Lydney until 1810 and Redbrook until 1816. (See also appendix 7: *Account 2.*)

# 8

# THE NINETEENTH CENTURY

Blast furnaces around Dean were producing pig iron, using charcoal, at the close of the eighteenth century, but industries in other parts of Britain were experimenting with coke-smelting. Eventually the iron industry gradually transferred its dependence from charcoal to good supplies of coke and the coalfields became important centres for the iron-smelting industry. Dean coal was not suitable for producing coke and that produced in the Welsh mines at Merthyr and Blainau was far superior. Given this situation there was no incentive for Dean ironmasters to change because they had ample supplies of charcoal, and that fuel continued to be used to the early years of the nineteenth century.

Furnaces procured coke by 'charking' coal in heaps, roughly similar to the manner used for the production of charcoal. Small coal was used as a fuel to produce steam power which was more reliable than the waterwheel but Parkend continued to use a large wheel until 1827. The introduction of coke and the use of steam engines and blowing cylinders, in place of bellows, resulted in improved designs of blast furnaces. At Bromley Hill, Soudley, Darkhill, Whitecliff and Parkend, sites were chosen where the terrain provided a natural height for charging the increased height of furnaces. At Cinderford small wagons had to be pushed up a slope to charge the furnace before improvements were made.

The quantity of heat carried through the furnace by ascending gases and the presence of a large quantity of inactive nitrogen resulted in attempts being made to reclaim some heat by raising the height of the furnaces from around 20ft (6.09m) to 30ft (9.14m) or more. Increased blast resulted in the number of tuyeres being raised from two to three. Higher levels of heat in the furnace led to the introduction of fireclay bricks – one benefit from the developing brick industry. The higher temperature of the coke blast furnaces enabled higher lime slags to be used, so less pure ore could be used and the problematical sulphur contained in the ore and fuel was absorbed by the slag. There was one problem with the higher temperatures and that was the reduction of silica to silicon which dissolved in the molten iron. On solidification the sow and pig iron became a coarse-grained graphite iron generally unsuitable for castings, when used direct from the furnace, and it had to be re-melted before use.

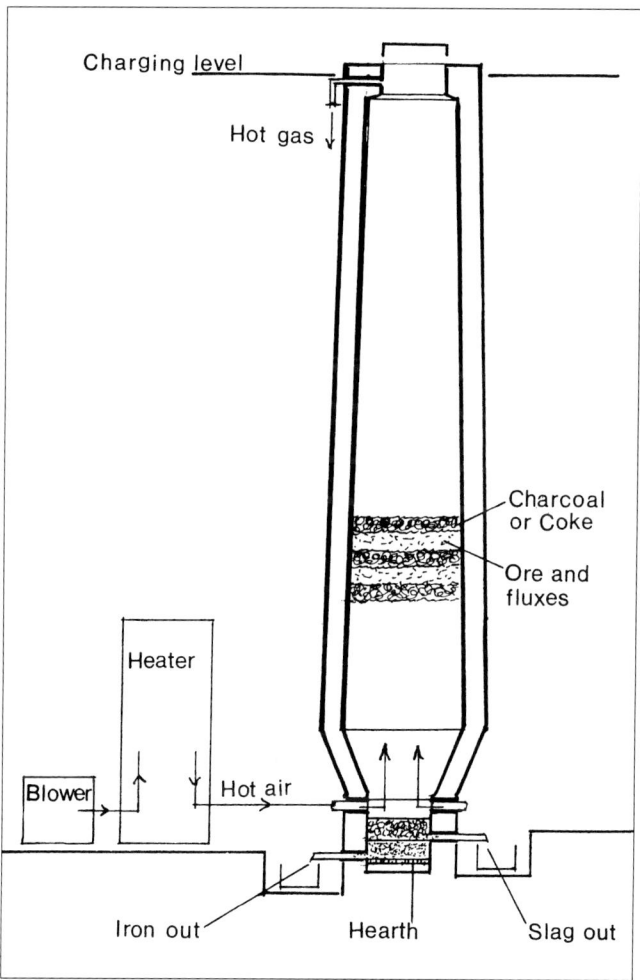

35 Diagrammatic representation of a later blast furnace particularly at a time when coke was replacing charcoal

The later blast furnace illustrated here (35) was most applicable to the change to the coke period. Conveyors would carry the ore, coke and fluxes, generally limestone, to the top of the furnace which was probably over 30ft (9.14m) high. Hot air at about 800 degrees Celsius would be blown into the brick-lined furnace causing the fuel to burn and produce carbon monoxide, which acted on the ore and raised its temperature to about 1600 degrees Celsius. The molten iron fell to the bottom and was drawn off and run into sand moulds to form pig iron. The molten slag floated on the iron and was drawn off and used in the manufacture of cement.

In 1795 the first coke blast furnace was built at a site near Cinderford Bridge. Ore was brought in on mules' backs and coke was made nearby in the open. Pig iron of good quality was produced but the output was less than 20 tons (20.3 tonnes) per week and it could not compete with iron from South Wales and Staffordshire and it closed, probably in 1806.

Samuel Botham, a Quaker from Uttoxeter, was in partnership with the brothers Bishton of Shifnal, Shropshire, and was persuaded to invest a

*36* Nineteenth-century iron miners. Each held a candle called a 'Nelly' in their mouths as their only form of light

*1* Iron ore broken down for smelting

*2* Dense ore 60 per cent iron rich

3 Crease Limestone showing its tunnels and cavities

4 Stalactitic goethite and calcite on Crease Limestone. © *Jonathan Wright*

5 Ochre from Clearwell Caves. ©
*Clearwell Caves*

6 Mining ochre in Clearwell Caves. ©
*Clearwell Caves*

7 Iron industry scowles in the Forest of Dean. © *Gloucestershre County Council 2004*

*8* Iron industry scowles near Coleford. © *Mark Walters, Dean Archaeological Group*

*9* Iron industry scowles at the 'Devil's Chapel', Bream. © *Dean Heritage Museum Trust*

*10* Building a charcoal stack. © *Forestry Commission*

*11* The preparation of charcoal. © *Peter Ralph*

*12* Harvesting charcoal. © *Peter Ralph*

13 Soudley Charcoal Furnace 1635, showing the furnace head and the iron discharge. © *Ian Gorton*

14 Soudley charcoal furnace 1635, showing the 22ft (6.7m) waterwheel. © *Ian Gorton*

15 Experiment in reconstructed shaft furnace. © *Peter Crew*

16 Excavated base of a shaft furnace. © *Peter Crew*

*17* Iron 'blooms' from the Forest of Dean. © *Peter Crew*

*18* Railway 'churn' in Old Ham Iron Mine. © *Roy Fellows*

*19* The gatehouse of St Briavels Castle

*20* Whitecliff Furnace. © *Dean Heritage Museum Trust*

*21* Tump House, Cinder Hill, home of David Mushet

*22* Remains of Darkhill Iron Works

*23* Wigpool Iron Mine. © *Dean Heritage Museum Trust*

24 Cannop Ponds – industrial water

25 Soudley Ponds – industrial water

*26* Free Miners crest in Newland church

27 Representation of iron miners tools on Abenhall church

28 *Above left:* Demonstration shaft furnace at Dean Heritage Centre. © *Dr Doug Gentles*
29 *Above right:* Demonstration charcoal stack at Dean Heritage Centre

principal share in some iron works in Gloucestershire. He came to live in Coleford and commenced constructing a coke-smelting blast furnace at Whitecliff on the west of Thurston's Brook, which runs through Coleford to Newland, and continues as the Valley Brook to Lower Redbrook and the Wye. Progress was good but, in 1799, deep snow led to a swelling brook flooding the project and causing significant damage. Botham's associates from South Wales refused to help him and, having lost his investment, he moved back to Uttoxeter. His associates, together with Thomas Halford and Moses Teague, took over the works and completed them in 1804. The blast was to be provided by steam raised by coke.

David Mushet's expertise in iron production was widely known and he was manager of Alfreton Iron Works in Derbyshire when, in 1808, Thomas Halford, a London stockbroker who owned the Whitecliff Works, contacted him to make visits to Whitecliff to advise on production methods and output with which he was displeased. That was why the brilliant Scot and early metallurgist came to Coleford. He became a partner at Whitecliff and purchased Tump House, later renamed Forest House, on Cinder Hill. Only for a relatively short time did David remain at the works for 'he had grave reasons for being most dissatisfied with his partner and he withdrew'. Perhaps Halford's usual habit of interfering with the works had become a problem and he certainly disliked the Foresters. He also had some differing opinions regarding dealing with the high price of coal and iron in the Forest against cheaper companies from outside. The culmination of these problems caused the termination of the partnership. Halford purchased Mushet's partnership and carried on with the works but became bankrupt in 1816 and the works were dismantled, except the furnace, which was left standing.

In 1810 David Mushet severed his connection with the Whitecliff Works, but stayed at Forest House. A little distance up the road from his house was a large stone barn where he, and later his eldest son Robert, carried out numerous experiments with iron. In 1815 he took out a patent on a process of producing 'refined iron' direct from the blast furnace without using the refinery. He had succeeded in producing an excellent quality of refined iron, virtually free from phosphorus and sulphur, and superior to that obtained in the ordinary refinery. In fact, some of the yield was steel and for 10 years he shaved with a pair of razors he made at the time.

By 1819 David was to build his own iron works on 6 acres (2.43ha) of Crown land he obtained from the Office of Woods, the Crown representative, by exchanging if for 2 acres (0.81ha) of land he owned elsewhere in the

*37* David Mushet (1772-1847)

Forest. His site was at Darkhill, on Gorsty Knoll, between Milkwall and Parkend and about 2 miles (3.2km) from Coleford. There was a brickworks on the site which he had already acquired. His works had two small furnaces initially and all attendant facilities including some workers' cottages. Later he built a larger furnace which was capable of taking 2.5 tons (2.54 tonnes) and he experimented with many batches, not only with the rich ore of the Forest but also with some from Cumberland. There was a public tramroad on the other side of the brickworks and a short connection provided access to the new works. He used the brickworks to make fire bricks, amongst other products, and the fire bricks were used to line many furnaces. With the advantage of this new process, which he had previously patented, he produced excellent-quality refined iron and he worked on his process for another two years, but it was not adopted in Wales or Staffordshire. Some 50 years later his son Robert said that it was the nearest process for making steel to Bessemer's and would have made that process unnecessary if only the temperature could have been kept higher.

In the 1820s a young man, Moses Teague, who had experienced some business misfortunes, decided to become involved in iron making. David had always held the view that good-quality cheap iron could not be

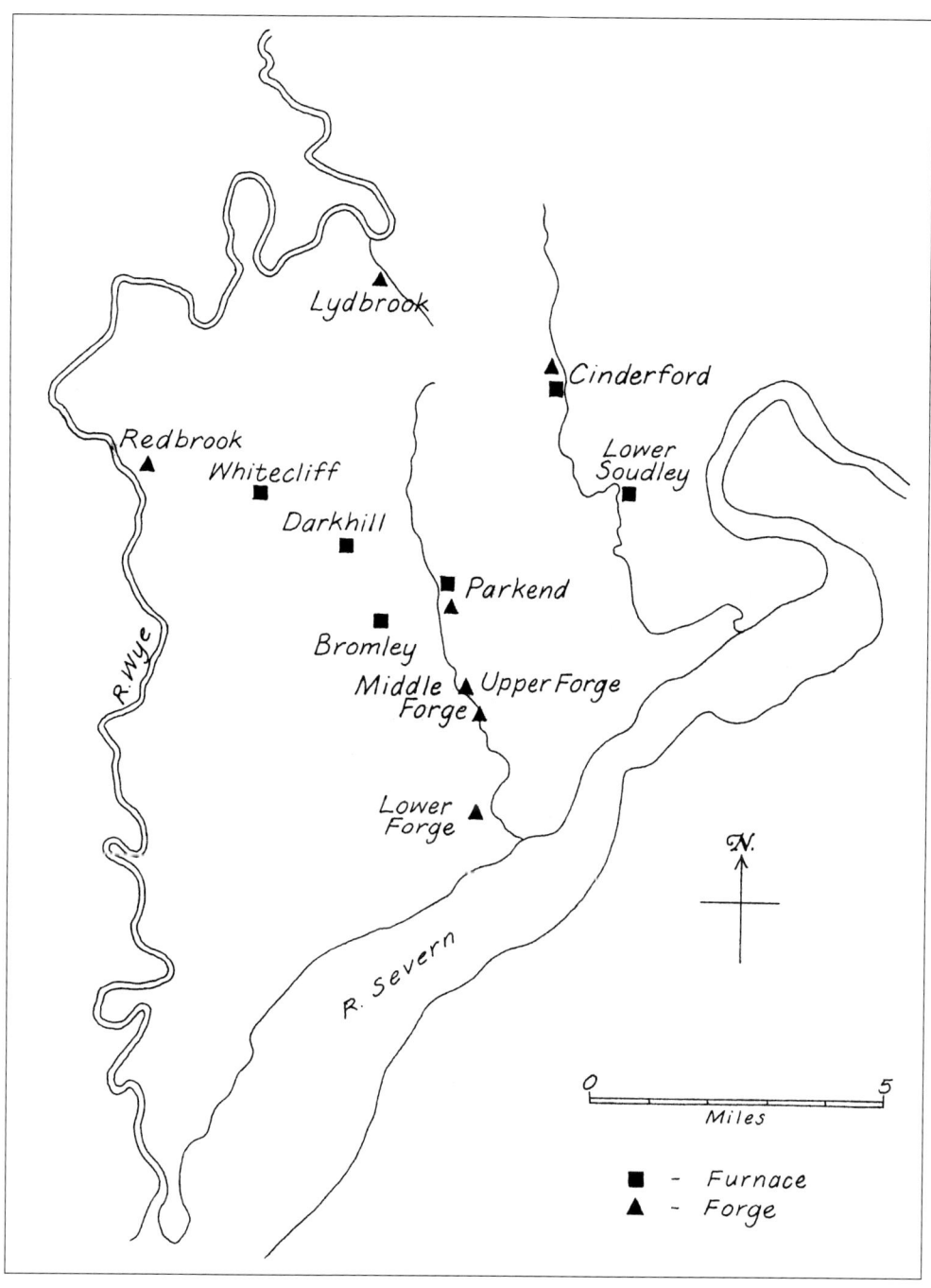

*38* Map of coke-era furnaces and forges in Dean

produced from Forest coal and iron ore because of the physical difficulties they presented. Moses Teague regarded this as a challenge and, such was David's conviction, that he allowed Moses to experiment with the use of his furnace, or cupola as some described it, at Darkhill. Moses did manage to make coke-smelted iron and, after further experiments 'at Mr Mushet's furnace' with coke of Low Delf coal, from the Bixslade Collieries, Edward Protheroe proposed to re-open his, probably improved, Parkend Furnace.

The effects of the Industrial Revolution brought major changes to the working families in the Forest. Until the later stages of the eighteenth century the men had been self-employed iron miners, colliers and quarrymen, working in small groups and seldom coming into contact with outsiders who they regarded as 'foreigners'. But the Forest was very rich in raw materials required by the new era of industrialisation in Britain. Coal and iron were in demand and it was inevitable the 'foreigners' would come in to take advantage of the availability of those materials. Supplies of iron ore had been won from sources at, or near, the surface but maybe the depletion of these areas had resulted in the import of ores by sea from Whitehaven. This was not an immediate problem as the Forest had limestone flux, water power and charcoal readily available, and despite some closures, it was still an important charcoal producing area achieving some 2600 tons (2642 tonnes) of iron per year. It is said that the Teagues were probably the only working family to concern themselves with the task of competing with the 'foreigners', and over the next generation had risen to be powerful businessmen. But outside the Forest industrial methods were changing. Abraham Derby had used coke in a blast furnace as early as 1709, and now the local industry was entering the coke-furnace, wire and tinplate era!

The need for a tramroad network was raised in the late 1700s and in 1801 Benjamin Outram, an engineer, reported that he would recommend the provision of tramroads through Dean to the rivers Severn and Wye. The system would be of value to the coal miners but also to the coke blast furnaces at Cinderford, Parkend and Lydney. Between 1809 and 1815 three tramroads were established; Lydney–Lydrook (Severn & Wye Railway & Canel Co.), Cinderford–Bullo (Pill Railway Co.) and Coleford–Monmouth (Monmouth Railway Co.). These tramroads were tracks for the passage of horse-drawn wagons and were extensively used by all Dean industries and had many later extensions.

Mushet was well before his time and had invested in coal and iron mines, brick making and tramroads. He was in support of Dean's tramroads at a very early stage by being amongst the subscribers listed in the original Acts of Parliament for the Lydney and Lydbrook Railway (1809) and the Monmouth Railway (1810). In 1825 he secured a licence for the Oakwood Tramroad and, in the same year, commenced driving an old and a new ore adit at Oakwood, winning 40-50,000 tons (40,640-50,800 tonnes) of ore. Of coal works in 1841 he held Old Furnace Level Gale, Hawlers Slade, Deep Engine, Protection Level, Bixslade Level, Bixslade Upper Level, Dark Hill and Shutcastle.

However, Mushet had joined the wealthy group of 'in-comers', so disliked by the Foresters, who would go to any lengths to protect their investments and income. In 1829 Moses Teague expressed his wish to introduce steam trains to the Forest with lines from Cinderford northward to Ross-on-Wye and southwards to the Severn port of Purton Pill. There was little objection to the northward lines but those to the south would enable Moses to sell coal from his Foxes Bridge pit and provide help and employment to local people where wages were low and unemployment widespread. Although the proposals did not interfere with areas served by existing tramroads they were perceived as a threat as they might encourage the opening of other pits which would provide unwelcome competition. An Act of Parliament would be required before completion of the scheme and Moses had the help of Charles Mathias, who would finance the operation and petition the House of Commons to allow him to bring in a Private Bill. David Mushet and Edward Protheroe, ex-MP and prominent coalmaster, formed the opposition. Moses and Charles Mathias attracted much support from the Foresters, but that is never on the credit side of an argument such as this and the efforts of David and Protheroe to delay Mathias's Bill led to it being defeated in March 1832! They had protected their income but denied steam trains being introduced to the Forest for many years.

Feelings among the Foresters towards the 'foreigners' like David Mushet, and the Crown, built up during the early decades of the nineteenth century and led to riots in the Forest in 1831. A Commission was appointed by the government in 1832 to examine the problems which had arisen. Low wages and unemployment were widespread among the miners' families and they took exception to 'foreigners' purchasing pits and mines, and saw this as a threat to free miner rights and privileges. The Crown increased their wrath by providing fenced-off areas for tree planting which denied them access to parts of the Forest, and prevented encroachment for building and cultivation. David was one who gave evidence to the Commission, stating

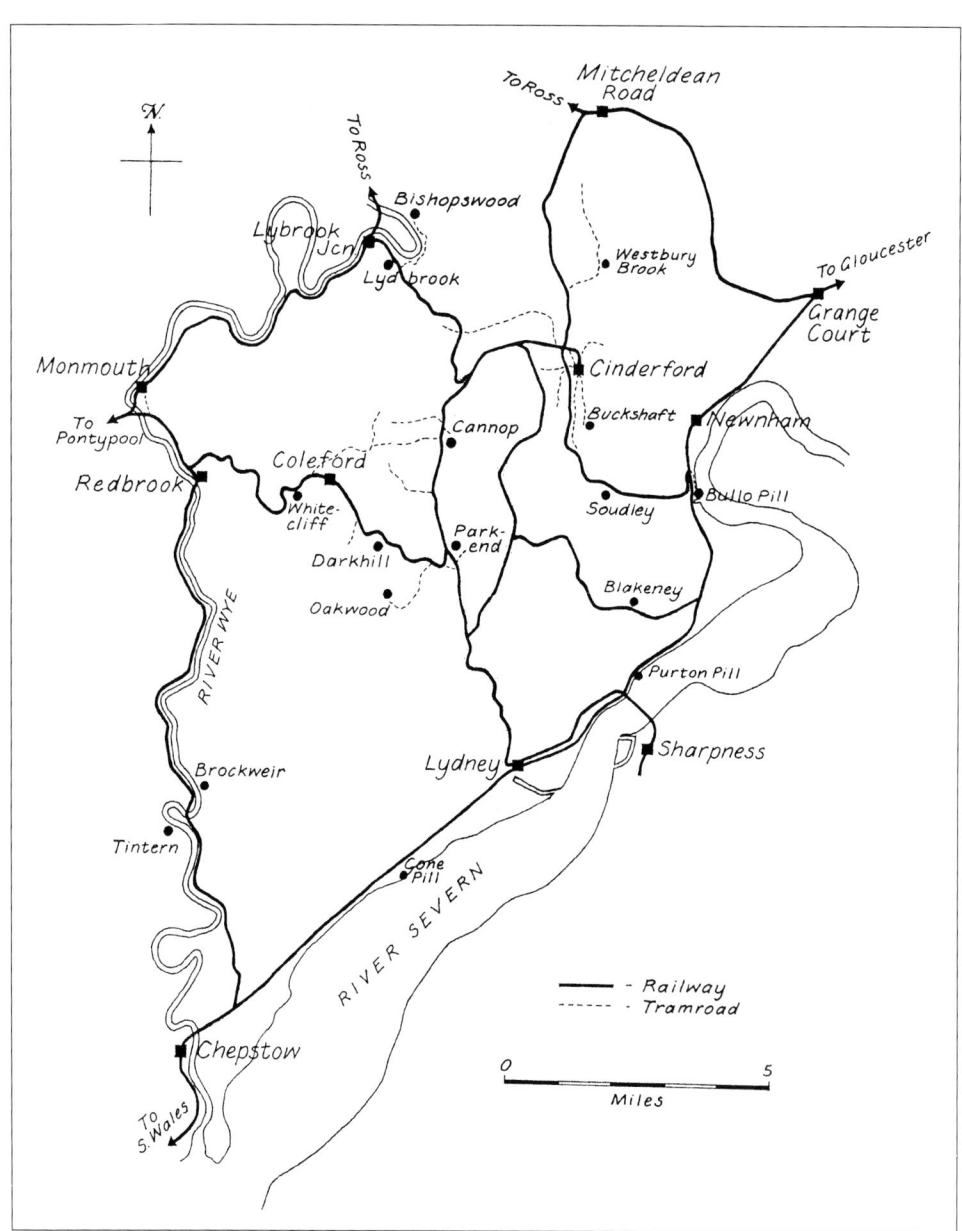

39 Layout of railways and tram roads

that their investment in pits, mines and tramroads had saved the Forest from 'depredation and waste' caused by the Foresters. The latter argued that rights to dig coal and ore in the Forest had been given to them 500 years before, and had been confirmed twice by the Crown since that time. In addition, the loss of their rights had started in 1777 when their Mine Law Court had been abolished.

The Commission published its report in 1835 and, in general, it was largely in favour of the 'foreigners'. There was fear among the Foresters that subsequent legislation might restrict the miners' rights so Robert Mushet, then 24, decided to work for a year and a day in the upper mine level at Oakwood Mill, digging iron ore, and so achieved his status as a free miner. The Dean Forest Mines Act was based on the Commission report, and confirmed the right of 'foreigners' to own their mines and pits but also stated that only free miners could take out new gales.

In 1841 David Mushet gave evidence to Elijah Waring, a London Inspector of the Children's Employment Commission, which had been appointed by the government to investigate the employment of children in certain industrial establishments in Britain. In view of the extent of industrial activity in the Forest it is, perhaps, surprising that he interviewed only 22 employers and managers of tinworks, iron works, coal pits and iron mines, and saw 13 children. He then interviewed three surgeons, two clergymen and four school teachers! Waring described David as 'a gentleman distinguished for his scientific acquirements and minute acquaintance with the mineral statistics of the Forest'. David was critical of the 'beer houses', because the men and boys were often drunk, and much in favour of Sunday Schools without, it seems, qualifying his support for them. But, without being specific about his iron mines, he said that boys crawled about 60 or 70yds underground carrying iron ore in 'billies' strapped to their backs, then climbed to the surface with their loads, sometimes by notches cut in the rock, and in other places by ladders. He did, however, admit that a boy had been killed in one of his mines by a collapse of coal.

It was found that no girls were employed below ground in Dean, and only one woman was, but Waring estimated that three-quarters of the boys in the area worked underground. One reason for boys being taken underground by their fathers, as soon as they could earn money, was because of the lamentably low rates of pay for the miners. An Act was subsequently passed, despite stern opposition from colliery and mine owners and landowners, who drew mining royalties, which forbade the

*40* A 'Billy' (top) and
a 'Nelly' (bottom)

employment of women and children underground but the government
had to appoint inspectors to enforce the legislation.

In 1845 David Mushet gave his Darkhill Iron Works, in equal shares, to
his three sons, William, David and Robert. A partnership agreement was
drawn up for the three brothers, whereby Robert was the sole manager of
The Darkhill Iron Co., styled Robert Mushet & Co., William's one third
share was soon mortgaged to Gratrex & Co, Bankers of Monmouth, as a
security for his debts. Robert and David carried out improvements to the
blast furnace property, including the introduction of hot blast, and David
was responsible for the design 'on the scientific principles of Mr J Gibbons'
of a new furnace which produced fine foundry iron. It should also be said
that the furnace project did introduce some dissent into the partnership.

In 1846 David Mushet lived in Monmouth and Robert had moved
into Forest House, Coleford. There was considerable dissent in the
family; William can be discounted, but there was strife between David

41 Robert Mushet
(1811–91)

junior and his brother Robert. In the meantime Robert had been experimenting in making a 'grey cast iron from an air furnace', which he achieved by combining rich ores with clay, lime and carbon into rough lumps which were then dried. These materials produced, by fusion in a small air furnace, a highly carburetted grey cast iron.

David Mushet senior, so justifiably described as 'The Man of Iron' died at Monmouth on 7 June 1847 and was buried at Staunton. In his later years he was dismayed by the unrest among his sons. There was a downturn in trade and Robert was aware of the financial difficulties they were encountering. Ultimately, David and Robert dissolved their partnership, David was to have the iron works, the Darkhill and Shutcastle coal levels and the Easter Iron Mine. Robert was to manage the brickyard and the coal levels of Bixslade, Howlers Slade and Old Furnace. The Darkhill Furnace was probably never used again. Robert went into partnership with Thomas Deykin Clare, a Birmingham merchant in a new venture – R Mushet & Co, Forest Steel Works. He had a small experimental steelworks, near Darkhill, which included a crucible furnace and a pair of old-fashioned wooden tilt hammers.

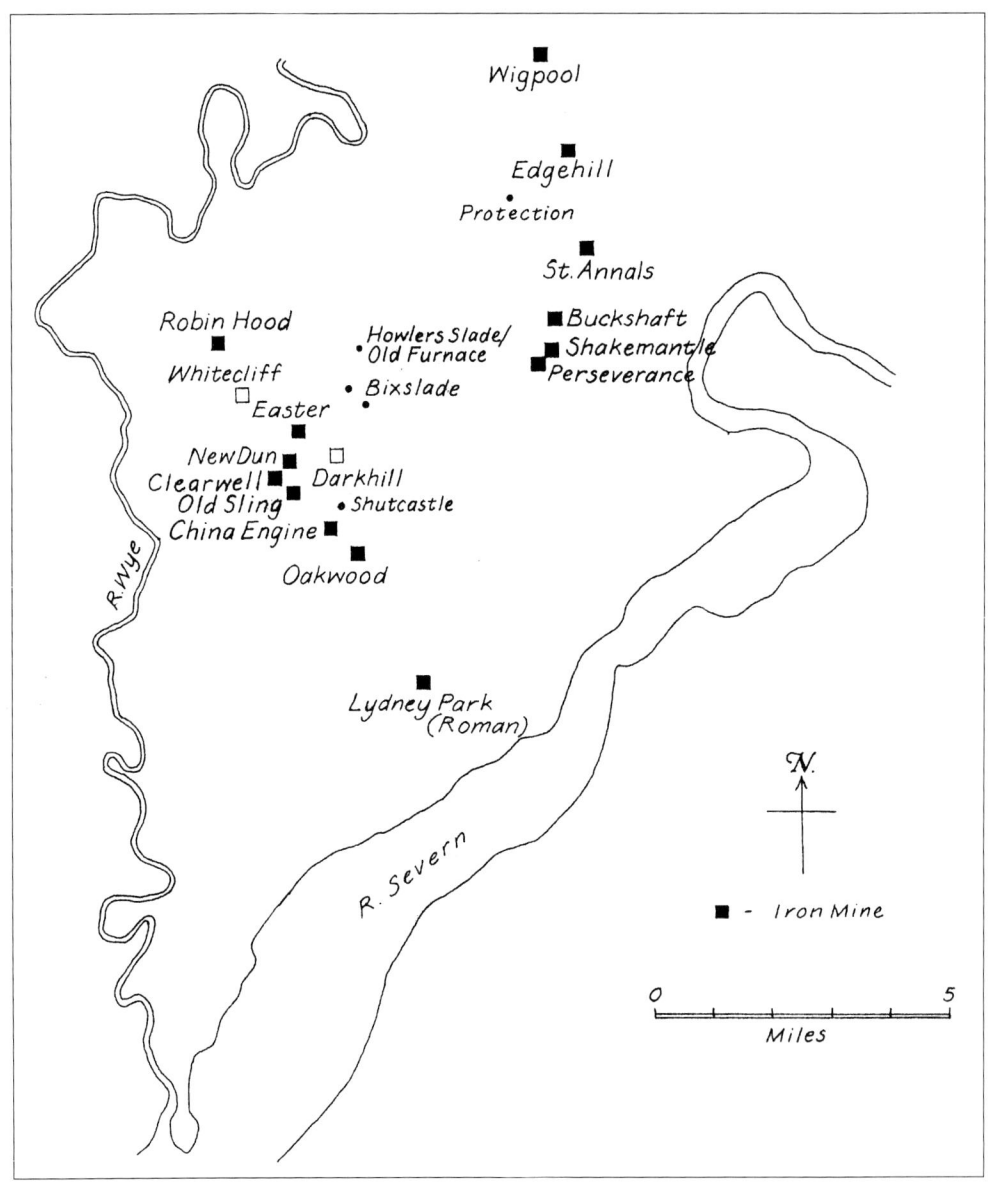

42 Distribution of principal iron mines and some associated coal mines

In 1856 Robert added a cupola for melting pig iron, a small Bessemer hearth and blowing apparatus. He was shown a sample of iron made by the Ebbw Vale Company, using the Bessemer process, and was asked by one of the Ebbw Vale partners if he could improve it. Recognising that the presence of excess oxygen was causing the trouble with this iron, Robert removed it by using a material known as spiegeleisen, a triple compound of iron, manganese and carbon which, when melted and added to the blown Bessemer metal, de-oxidised it successfully. In 1888 William Crawshay paid Robert the very high compliment when he said that a piece of iron submitted to him was 'the very best I ever saw in my life'.

In 1862 The Titanic Steel & Iron Co. Ltd was formed and a large works were built near the Darkhill premises. By 1868 Robert was producing his self-hardening tool steel which was much in demand in Sheffield. It was made by alloying it with tungsten and it produced hard, tough, durable steel which hardened itself without quenching, and a fine cutting edge could be applied to tools immediately. The trade moved out of the carbon-steel field and tungsten-alloy steels, although in a more advanced stage, are still manufactured throughout Britain.

All seemed well with the Titanic Company until 1871 when the works was closed and the company voluntarily wound up in 1874. About 400 tons (406 tonnes) of old iron was purchased in 1871 by Richard Thomas & Co. of the Lydney Tinplate Works. Robert Forester Mushet had 20 years of retirement before he died at Cheltenham in January 1891 in his eightieth year. So the Man of Steel, and indeed of Bessemer-Mushet steel, was gone.

In late 1827 Moses Teague, with William Montague, Church and Fraser, formed the first Cinderford Iron Co. Building works began and, in the following year, negotiations for a weighing machine began with the Forest of Dean Railway. Lack of finance delayed completion until late 1829 but, despite the depression in the iron industry, the works operated until October 1832. Three years later, in 1835, Teague induced William Allaway (who, with his sons, Stephen and William, was engaged in the tinplate trade at Lydbrook) to join with William Crawshay of Cyfarthfa, William Montague and John Pearce (partner of Allaway at Lydbrook) in forming the second Cinderford Iron Company to resuscitate the Works.

Much iron was forwarded to Lydbrook but, in 1837, an internal crisis arose which was explained in a letter from Crawshay to Allaway. The principal difficulty appeared to be the concern that water accumulating in

*43* Cinderford Iron Works, a coke iron blast furnace *c.*1875

Bennett's collieries could, at any time, submerse Mr Protheroe's collieries and thereby deny the Cinderford Works their supply of coal. It was also held that Cinderford owed the Lydbrook Tinplate Works an amount of money and Crawshay settled that amount with Allaway. Their problems were resolved but Crawshay proposed that, in future, a manager should be appointed for Cinderford, having no connection with either partner, to keep the two concerns completely separate. In 1838 Thomas Prichard, of Ross, agreed a nominal lease with a view to sale to William Allaway, William Crawshay and others, of 14 acres (5.6ha) bounded on the west by Cinderford Brook, and on which stood the Cinderford Iron Works. The sale was also to include the veins of coal in the Lower Bilson Colliery and others. At about the same time Peter and James Teague agreed to a lease which was aimed at a sale to Allaway, Crawshay and their associates, of the coal mine and gale called Water Engine, near Daniels Ford, and all buildings of the Cinderford Iron Works, in the name of John Addis and Edward Protheroe, and then in trust to Peter and James Teague. The sale included veins of coal known as the Lower Bilson Colliery. These agreements were very complex but it emerged that the iron works site was owned by Prichard and the Teagues and a sale would secure the tenure of the works.

Accounts for 1847 to 1849 indicate that this prosperous works was jointly owned by William Crawshay and William Allaway, with Henry, Crawshay's second son, as manager. David Mushet junior paid a serious compliment to the cold-blast iron ore of Cinderford, saying 'that it brings a high price in the market – its tenacity adapting it, in a high degree, for cast hardware and tinplate'. By 1858 there were four blast furnaces at Cinderford, three always in blast, and producing some 500 hundred tons (508 tonnes) of finest hot-blast iron each week. The ore came chiefly from the Milkwall district, to the west of the Forest, and from Shakemantle, Buckshaft and St Annal's on the eastern side. With three blast furnaces in operation, the annual output of iron during the two years to June 1840, was 12,000 tons (12,195 tonnes). From the peak of having three furnaces always in blast performance fell to two in blast in 1876-9, and dwindled to one at reduced capacity with the works finally closing in 1894.

Tinplate was originally sheet iron, and later sheet steel, covered with a protective layer of tin. In the 1660s Andrew Yarranton obtained much information on its manufacture when he visited Saxony. He realised that Cornish tin miners and Forest iron miners were both in a distressed condition, which could be relieved by the manufacture of tinplate. In an experiment many thousands of plates were made using Dean iron and Cornish tin. They proved superior to German plates as the Forest iron was tough and flexible. Despite the impressive results of the experiment no commercial development followed. It was not until the eighteenth century that tinplate was produced at Redbrook in 1774, at Lydbrook in 1798 and at Lydney around 1810.

Tinplate works, using coke as fuel, were started in South Wales in the early nineteenth century. Coke slowly replaced charcoal in Dean as Townshend & Wood commenced manufacture at Redbrook, the Pidcocks or John James at Lydney and the Partridges and Allaways at Lydbrook. In the early 1870s Richard Thomas followed at Lydbrook and Lydney. Then James and Greenham opened works at Parkend, and so did Chivers and Bright at Hawkwell. In 1880 the five established works were comprised of 17 mills of which 15 were working, and producing around 351,000 boxes per year. A great part of the production was exported to America, and some un-tinned black plates were sent to America for varnishing, then returned for use in the photographic industry.

The iron plates had to be cleaned of ferric oxide and other impurities before they were tinned. The Cannop Chemical Works made sulphuric acid using sulphur from Sicily, but the cheaper alternative was the acid as a waste product of the Swansea copper works, although it did contain some impurities, of which one was arsenic.

In 1834 the Lydbrook Tinplate Works were put up for sale but in 1847-9 they were still operated by the Allaways. In 1850 the name changed to Allaways, Partridge & Co. and they were still buying cordwood for charcoaling from the Office of Woods. They tried to persuade the Severn and Wye Railway to convey tinplate from Lydbrook to Lydney by tramroad but negotiations were unsuccessful and products continued to be sent via the Wye to Bristol. In 1871 the works were leased to Richard Thomas, who was to make a great impact on the Forest's industrial growth, and he then moved to a residence in Lydbrook.

In 1875 Richard Thomas's company acquired the Lydney Tinplate Works. By 1880 there were five mills at Lydbrook of which four were working with an average weekly production of 450 boxes from each mill. In 1882 there was a problem with water levels in Trafalgar, Speculation and Old Bob's Collieries and Thomas's company suffered loss in liquidation with Francis Brain and Partners. Richard bought the Lydbrook Colliery in 1877 and later he owned Speculation and he opened the Waterloo Colliery in 1882. By 1883 the Lydbrook Works were closed and the company was in liquidation – the Gloucester Banking Co. were the mortgagees and in possession of the assets. The company made a quick recovery and were solvent by early 1884, and later that year Richard Thomas & Co, Lydbrook and Lydney Works were registered as a limited company with Richard well supported by his sons, Richard Beaumont and Frank. After the McKinley Tariff of 1890, which limited trade with the USA, the market difficulties caused a recession, but in 1893 the plant comprised five mills. A temporary closure took place in 1899, again due to market difficulties. In their most prosperous years their workforce totalled around 700.

There is no certainty that tinplate works existed at Lydney when David Tanner acquired them in 1781, and the more probable answer is that there was the manufacture of plate for tinning. The Pidcocks obtained the lease in 1790 and put it up for auction in 1810, but the property was withdrawn at the auction. Negotiations between the Pidcocks and others were abortive and, in 1813, the Pidcocks assigned their Lydney interests to the Rt. Hon Charles Bathurst who leased them to John James of the Redbrook

Tinplate Works in 1814. By 1824 James had constructed The New Mills on Bathurst's land standing just above the Norchard Colliery. In 1841 James's 'Middle Rolling Mill' comprised two pairs of Tinplate Rolls driven by a waterwheel in winter assisted by a steam engine in summer, and capable of converting 20 tons (20.32 tonnes) of bar-iron weekly. From 1845 John and Henry James took a new lease on the property for 12 years.

The James's surrendered their lease to Charles Bathurst in 1847 and he re-leased it to the Allaways of Lydbrook Tinplate Works. They had three forges, mills and a tin-house and produced 1200 boxes of tinplate a week. Similar works, only larger, were carried out at Lydney by the Allaways and they produced about 1000 boxes a week besides some sheet iron.

William Allaway & Sons surrendered lease on the Lydney premises to Richard Thomas & Sons of Lydbrook in 1875 when the plant comprised four mills. In 1882 Thomas was fined for smoke nuisance and built a 164ft (50m) high stack to abate it. Early in 1883 the works closed due to Richard Thomas & Sons' financial difficulties and the company went into liquidation. By early 1884 the company were solvent again and Richard became managing director of Richard Thomas & Co. to operate Lydney and Lydbrook Works. He was succeeded by his son, R. Beaumont Thomas in 1888 and the Thomas's tinplate manufacturing interests greatly increased.

Parkend had a long history of a furnace and a forge although these were suppressed in 1674. However, it was not until 1799 that a furnace using coke was erected about half a mile (0.81km) lower down the valley than the former one, and operated by a Mr Perkins. The works were eventually sold to John Protheroe and he passed them to his nephew, Edward Protheroe, ex-MP for Bristol, and a prominent owner of several collieries in the neighbourhood. Following Moses Teague's experiment in smelting with a coke, Protheroe was prepared to re-open the, probably improved, works but he granted a lease of the furnace and premises to the Forest of Dean Iron Company, of which Moses was a member. In 1826 William Montague and John James of Lydney became the sole lessees, and they erected a second furnace in 1827, powered by an immense undershot waterwheel of 51ft (15.55m) diameter, 6ft (1.83m) width and weighing 60 tons (60.96 tonnes), said to be one of the largest in Britain.

Two extension ponds, the Cannop Ponds, were formed higher up the Parkend–Cannop Valley, by damming the Newerne stream, and directing water to the furnace by a leat. However, these ponds were not particularly effective and complaints arose that the damming had seriously reduced the water level in the Lydney canal. A steam engine was installed for creating the necessary blast but was insufficient and, in 1849, another engine of 90hp was installed to power the 45ft (13.72m) high furnaces. There then came a depression in the iron trade, and this was principally the cause of the two furnaces not being worked together. In 1841 only one furnace was working, powered by water in summer and a steam engine in winter. To the end of 1840, 60 tons (60.96 tonnes) was produced each week rising to 101 tons (102.6 tonnes) in 1841, and achieving an annual production of about 3640 tons (3698 tonnes) per year.

In 1843 the iron works had been out of blast for one and a half years, but they were again in use by the end of 1846. David Mushet, junior, was complimentary about the quality of railway girders produced by the plant, marvelling at the degree of deflection achieved under load before any failure occurred. Montague died in 1847 and James became the sole lessee. He installed another steam engine but used both coke and charcoal for power. He purchased the freehold from Protheroe in 1854 and then both furnaces were worked together under the management of Charles Greenham, who had also completed the construction of a new enterprise near the furnaces – iron forges, rolling mills and tinplate works. In 1864 the Forest of Dean Iron Company was producing about 280 tons (284 tonnes) of pig iron in a week and consuming, in the same period, 350 tons (355 tonnes) of coke and 600 tons (609 tonnes) of iron ore. They employed around 300 men, besides colliers, and were building another furnace. In 1871 all three furnaces were in blast, but one for only three months and, in the period around 1875, only two were in blast. In that year Edwin Crawshay purchased the Parkend plant, including the tinplate works. The three furnaces were capable of producing 600 tons (609 tonnes) of pig iron a week, but trade slumped and the works were closed in 1877.

The Parkend Tinplate Works were later operated by the Allaways who found employment for some 200 men who produced 500 boxes of tinplate per week. Two thirds of the iron they used in the works was obtained in the Forest. On a larger scale similar works were carried out at Lydney by William Allaway and Sons. There were five works at Lydney: the Lower Mill, the Lower Forge, the Middle Forge, the Upper Mill and the Upper Forge. Around 400 men were employed and they produced some 1000 boxes of tinplate every week besides a quantity of sheet iron. Materials for these works, including cordwood for conversion to charcoal, were supplied by the Forest.

The last charcoal iron for making tinplate was rolled at Lydney in 1886, as steel had superseded puddle iron for the work. In 1887 the yearly traffic between the Upper and Lower Forges was some 4200 tons (4267 tonnes) in process of manufacture, and 5200 tons (5283 tonnes) of coal to or from the New Mills. Down the Thomas's tramway from Lower Forge were conveyed tinplates in boxes to their wharf at the head of the canal. Horses worked the flat-bottomed wagons and a small steam boat, the Black Dwarf, carried the plates to Avonmouth from where they were shipped to places as far away as Australia. The Upper Forge was dismantled by 1890 and dismantling of the Middle Forge quickly followed. The production of tinplate was then carried on by Richard Thomas & Co. Ltd at the Lower Mills at Lydney. They were given a new lease by the Bathursts in 1889 and four years later their plant comprised eight mills.

Redbrook was producing tinplate in 1774 when the Lower Works were owned by Townshend and Wood. In 1790 the premises were sold to David and William Tanner of Tintern and Monmouth. Until 1800 the Lower Tinplate Works and the smaller Upper Works were run as one enterprise in which the Tanners improved the plant and premises as well as the forge up the Valley Brook. In 1791 the Tanners had financial difficulties and mortgaged

*44 Black Dwarf at Lydney Harbour*

the Lower Works to James Sevier of Bristol, manufacturer of horsehair, for £2200. David Tanner leased a dwelling and premises, previously the Upper Copper Works, to supplement his Lower Tinplate Works. For a while he prospered but financial difficulties resulted in him being declared bankrupt in 1798, and the Lower Tinplate Works were taken over by William Cowley and John James for the sum of £700 annually. It was said that litigation caused the works to become desolate by 1802, and they were put up for sale, but Cowley and James were still manufacturing tinplate in the Lower Works in 1805. The Upper Tinplate Works were leased to Robert Thompson who had probably produced tinplate there before 1818.

John James, a partner in the Lower Redbrook Works, acquired Lydney Tinplate Works in 1814, and ran both for a time but then seemed to abandon the Redbrook Works. These works were taken over by a B. Whitehouse, who repaired them and took over a lease for them in 1827. He also then became the occupier of the forges at Monmouth. Around this time a culvert was constructed to bring water from Upper Redbrook southwards to the first pond above the Lower Tinplate Works, and an adit to supplement the water supply was driven northwards from the top of the first pond. By 1842 the tinplate works had become the property of Philip Jones, who offered them for sale. Once again there was action relating to dilapidations and it was not until 1858 that the works were re-opened under David Griffiths as manager. In 1876 the works, still having two rolling mills, were operated by The Redbrook Tin Plate Co. The works were considerably enlarged following the opening of the Wye Valley Railway in 1876 and by 1880 there were three rolling mills each producing some 450 boxes a week. The works closed in 1883 but re-opened in 1884 with Daniel Horton as the superintendent. During the winter of 1898-9 the McKinley tariff resulted in the closure of the works, but two of the mills restarted in 1899.

Soudley had been occupied by iron works since 1565 with a main furnace being constructed in 1635. At one stage the Joneses of Hay Hill conducted wire works where wire was drawn by hand. Works continued until 1828 when Todd, Jeffries and Spirrin converted part of them to a paint and brassworks. In 1837 Edward Protheroe erected two blast furnaces, and operated them for four years before selling them to Benjamin Gibbons in 1857. Subsequently they were owned by a Mr Goold, who operated one furnace in blast using South Wales coke, producing about 20 tons (20.32 tonnes) of Forest iron at each casting.

Lydbrook had two busy centres of iron works called the Upper and the Lower respectively. The second of these was situated near the Wye and was once the property of the Foleys. They then passed to a Mr Partridge and were worked in connection with a furnace at Bishopswood. They were leased by Allaway in 1817 when they were composed of three forges, rolling and bar mills, and tin-house complete, capable of producing 100-150 boxes of tinplate per week. Later they were managed by Allaway's sons and the works then yielded 600 boxes per week which were despatched on the Wye. The iron used was chiefly from Cinderford as it was found to be the best suited for the purpose. The Upper Works were operated by Edward Russell, who improved them to employ about 100 men, manufacturing wire for fencing and telegraph purposes at a rate of 40-50 tons (40.64-50 8 tonnes) per week. They also made charcoal iron for horse nails and smith's work. Other works, resembling those described here, were carried on by James Russell at the Forest Vale Iron Works near Cinderford. They supplied considerable quantities of iron rods for telegraphic purposes and other wire as well as chain cable iron.

The coke blast furnace period began in Dean in 1795 and ended in 1894, thus terminating a history of iron-smelting which had begun before Roman times. Once again we have an intermittent life of an industry in the Forest but it covered the following periods: 1795-1894 at Cinderford, 1799-1877 at Parkend, 1807-15 at Whitecliff, 1819-62 at Darkhill, 1837-77 at Lower Soudley and 1856-65 at Bromley.

From 1874 the industry had declined and, after 1878, only two furnaces were in blast, both owned by Crawshays at Cinderford. By 1890 there was only one furnace in blast and the Crawshays were finally blown out in April 1894. Until 1856 Dean's iron-smelting industry had slowly adapted to changing conditions. By that year Bessemer discovered a method of converting cast iron into steel but needed a low phosphorus ore of which very little existed in Britain. However, a process by R.F. Mushet, using manganese in a compound, to remove the occluded oxygen obviated the need for ores with very low phosphorus content. Dean had low phosphorus ores but no longer held that advantage, and improvements in the industry made it possible to use low grade ore from other parts of the country thus negating Dean's overall advantage.

In 1780 George Wyrral referred to the stamping, or crushing, of blast furnace slag, called 'scruff', for the glass industry when he said:

The scoria which rises upon the surface of the metal by the present method of melting the iron ore in large furnaces is quite destitute of metal, and consisting of a vitreous substance more or less mixed with the impurities carried off with it in its fluid state. The best of it is used as an ingredient in the making of common green glass.

The 'stampers' were powered by waterwheels and pounded the vitreous substance to powder while separating out amounts of granulated iron, tagged lumps which were called 'shot', and scrap iron. The latter 'waste' items of iron were collected up and worked up with pig iron at the furnaces. Therefore the stampers had a dual role in providing material for the Bristol glass industry and sorting iron waste for 'recycling'. It is understood that bloomery slag was not used because of the high iron content. Charcoal blast furnace slags for dark green glass and cold-blast coke slags for lighter green and cream glass were suitable. During the nineteenth century, waterwheels powered stampers at Parkend, Tintern and two at Redbrook. David Mushet commented that the superior quality of the Bristol 'black bottles' was attributed to the use of a portion of slags from the charcoal furnaces of Dean.

# EPILOGUE

Mining of iron ore decreased towards the end of the nineteenth century from 199,111 tons (202,297 tonnes) in 1871 to 63,748 tons (64,768 tonnes) in 1891. West Dean had formerly sent large quantities of ore to South Wales and Staffordshire but, with the reduced output, large shipments were coming in from Spain. The Oakwood Valley had enjoyed commercial prosperity until the Oakwood and China operations closed in 1884 and 1892 respectively. These were two large and productive mines on the west of Dean.

On the east of Dean, Edgehill had produced 958,000 tons (973,328 tonnes) between 1843 and its abandonment in 1893. Six years later, in 1899, Shakemantle, Buckshaft and St Annal's closed, having produced 1,650,000 tons (1,676,400 tonnes) since 1841. Perseverance also closed at this time, the main reason being the closure of the Cinderford Furnaces in 1894.

From 1894 mining production continued to fall – from 9769 tons (9925 tonnes) in 1901 to 5830 tons (5923 tonnes) in 1911. There was a temporary resurgence during the period 1914-8 where seven mines produced 22,990 tons (23,358 tonnes), and in which the Easter, New Dun and Wigpool mines were engaged. Some production continued until 1925 but mining almost came to an end in that year. Looking back on the total performance it is significant that, from 1842, the western area had produced 1,135,000 tons (1,153,160 tonnes) of ore and the eastern area over 3,000,000 tons (3,048,000 tonnes).

There are several reasons for production dwindling to the low level of the 1920s. Deposits of ore were becoming exhausted above water level in the mines and it was therefore difficult to achieve uniformity in consignment when the product was variable in character. The additional

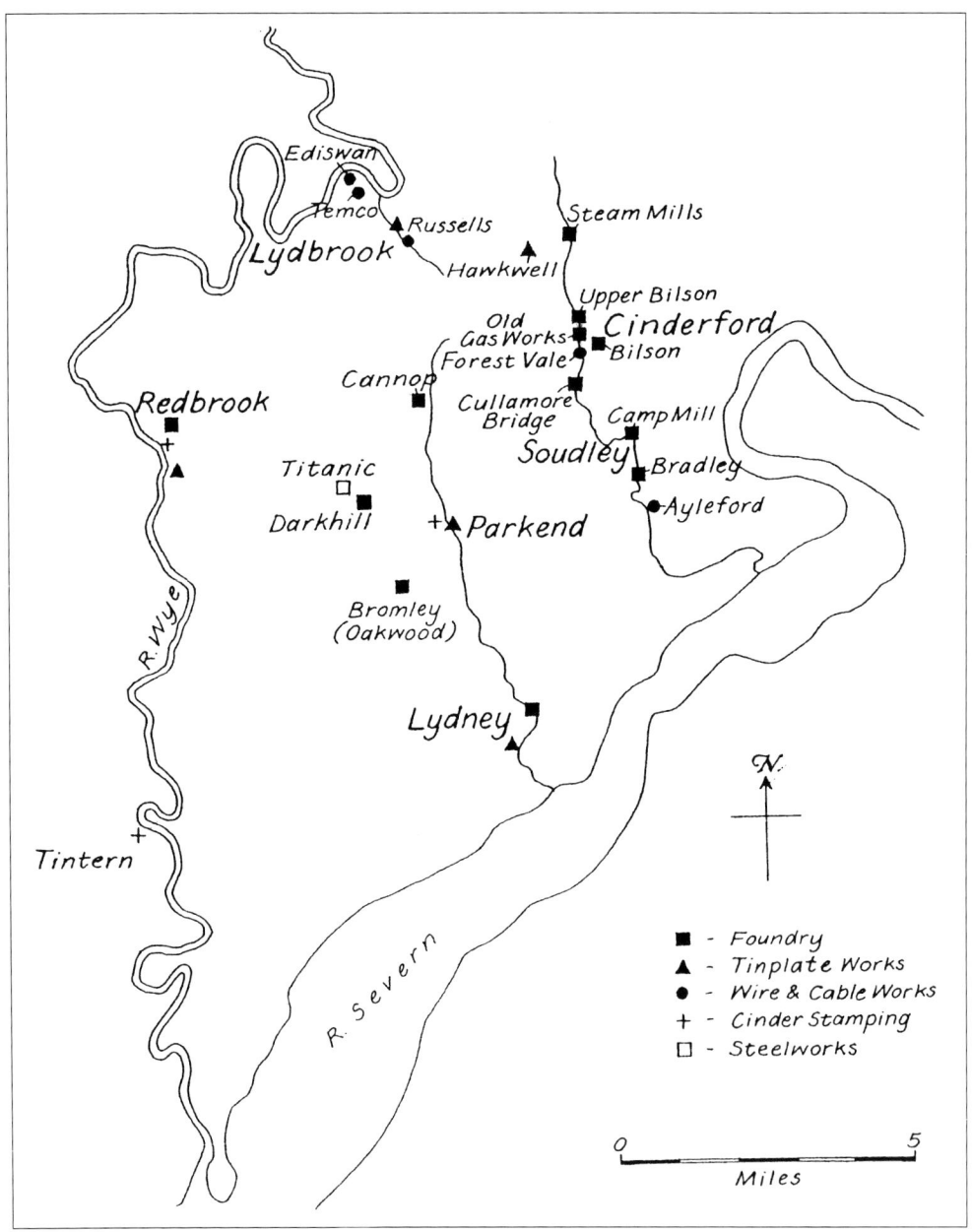

45 Map of the iron and steel industries in Dean in the nineteenth and twentieth centuries

pressure was obviously the imported Spanish ore which was arriving in ever larger quantities. In 1925 there was a proposal to resuscitate the industry by de-watering some of the mines and in 1926 Captain Pringle, a local mine owner, submitted a scheme to the Deputy Gaveller by which some mines on the eastern side could be de-watered via the Shakemantle shaft. The proposal was duly presented to the Forestry Commission with an estimate that some 5,000,000 tons (5,080,000 tonnes) of ore, of varying grades, could be recovered. In June 1930 the free miners sought the help of Ramsey MacDonald, Prime Minister, the Lord Privy Seal and their MP, asking for a Commissioner to attend at Coleford to hold an enquiry and determine the possibility of governmental finance being available to help de-water the mines. No finance was forthcoming so no new mining was possible on the east side. On the west side some production was achieved during the Second World War but, by then, mining had virtually ceased.

It is important to record that an estimate of the total production of iron ore from the Dean, from the beginning to the termination of mining, was probably more than 10,000,000 tons.

Some industries survived into the twentieth century. Bilson 'Gas Works' Foundry was still in operation and continued to produce castings by John Wheeler. Steam Mills continued and employed around 50 men and Heywood, near Cinderford, had made brass castings but then used iron only. The Redbrook Tinplate Co. had improved their works in 1867 and in 1944 electricity replaced water and coal for power. Their plate was the thinnest obtainable and they exported it worldwide. They went into liquidation in 1956-7 and the works were closed in 1961, being the last victim of the giant modern strip mills. From 1886 Lydney was producing tinplate and, at the outset of the Second World War, they were requisitioned by the Admiralty until 1946 then sold to the Steel Company of Wales in 1947 and closed in 1957. Lydbrook Cable Works had experience of making leads for fuses etc. at the turn of the nineteenth century and, in 1906, a German machine was purchased which covered six wires at a time with bitumen insulation. The same machine was still working in 1954! In 1912 a new works was built near Lydbrook Junction and, in 1914, contracts were secured for field telephone cables. Serious financial difficulties followed the First World War and the works were sold in 1925 but continued production until 1966.

The traditional method of burning charcoal did not die out completely with the demise of the iron works, and an account of the method was given in Chapter 1 by Edward Roberts. Just before the First World War a wood distillation works was built at Speech House Road. The plant, including a large single retort, was built in Germany and the installation was supervised by German technicians in 1913. Only the production of charcoal, grey acetate of lime, wood-spirit and wood-tar were contemplated in the original works but the basic task of producing charcoal and its derivatives has continued to recent times. Edward Roberts made charcoal in the open for the first three years of the Second World War, after which he was put in charge of batteries of charcoal-burning portable metal kilns, large steel drums with removable lids and a chimney, which were regarded as an unskilled method of producing charcoal. Edward Roberts returned to normal burning for a few years after the war but his death brought to an end a sight which had been characteristic of Dean for over two millennia.

The iron industry was symptomatic of the immense natural wealth of the Forest of Dean and its important contribution to our history must never be forgotten.

# APPENDIX 1

# ROMANO-BRITISH SITES AT CHESTNUTS HILL AND POPES HILL, FOREST OF DEAN

N.B. To fully appreciate the range of sites discussed in the appendices that follow interested parties may wish to purchase the Ordnance Survey map, Outdoor Leisure 14, which covers the Wye Valley and Forest of Dean.

In 1953, when the East Dean Council was laying a main to supply water to the Popes Hill district, Roman pottery was unearthed at two points by the contractor. Both occurrences were investigated by the archaeological section of the Forest of Dean Local History Society. The first occurrence was on the northern slope of Chestnuts Hill and was found when a spillway to the head tank was cut down the slope. At this point there occurs a rough semi-circular platform bounded on the downhill (northern) side by a slight retaining bank. When the spillway was cut across this platform a hut floor paved with large local flagstones, measuring about 5 x 3ft (1.5m x 0.9m) with some evidence of post holes, was encountered. Numerous sherds of Roman pottery, including Samian ware, were dug up, especially towards the edge or lower part of the platform. One of these, a bead rim dish of pseudo-Samian ware, belongs to the third to the fourth centuries. Below the hut floor there was much evidence of charcoal fires. Within the platform area there was also a circular depression which had the appearance of a filled-up well. That this was the explanation was proved by its excavation by Dr H. Selby who followed it down, through the Old Red Sandstone strata, for 17ft (5.18m) when water was reached. Some of the original stone revetting still remained in places. Portions of a glass wine flagon of about 1740-50, as well as a large medieval doubly-cordoned jug or pitcher, green glazed inside, were recovered. Pieces of wood from deep in the well proved, on examination at Kew, to be maple and ash. The former was very well preserved.

This site had been covered by oak forest until it was cut down in 1944. The woodland was planted in about 1800 and there are no records of previous afforestation. There is evidence here in the hut floor, the platform or garden enclosing the well and the pottery, of occupation, perhaps by shepherds or iron workers, covering a period stretching from Romano-British times to the mid-eighteenth century.

The other occurrence of Roman pottery was where the main passed on the south side of the Popes Hill Road. Here the trench revealed a shallow depression with a well-marked black occupation layer. Numerous trenches were dug over and around this occupation layer which lay on a slope facing southwards. The top layers revealed evidence of recent occupation and of paths surfaced by stones through the area which is now more or less common land. At depths of about 1ft (0.3m) and over, Roman pottery and iron slag in abundance were encountered. When the shallow depression occupation layer was cleared there was evidence of a hut dwelling of about 22ft (6.7m) in length and 9ft (2.74m) in width. This evidence consisted of some stone-ringed post holes, a slightly dished, rammed earth floor, with a hearth ringed with stones at one side, and with much stiff red clay surrounding the periphery of the floor. Several pieces of daub were encountered so that probably the dwelling was formed of wattle and daub sides tapering to a ridge pole roof, while the bases of the sides were embanked in stiff red clay as a seal. No doubt the daub debris from the sides of the hut tended to enhance the occurrence of peripheral red clay. The entrance to this hut would appear to have been at the south-eastern corner for the ground here was surfaced with a pitching of flat stone.

About 18ft (5.48m) to the west of the hut site, and on somewhat higher ground, a dished rectangular floor, roughly 3ft (0.9m) by 2ft (0.6m) of large stone slabs, was uncovered and on and around it, large quantities of iron slag. This slag was ubiquitous over the whole site but especially concentrated at this point. It was therefore concluded that the slabs were the base of a furnace for the reduction of iron ore, and the abundance of stiff red clay around this spot would have supplied the material necessary for building the furnace upper parts. Probably the occurrence of a stratum of red clay here over Old Red Sandstone shale was, along with the proximity of forest trees to supply charcoal, a major factor in determining the location of an iron-smelting furnace at this spot. A spring in which Roman sherds were found occurs lower down the slope and this could have supplied the necessary water for washing the iron slag and puddling the red clay. Scowl holes on the Cinderford ridge at no great distance away show that the Romans mined ore in the neighbourhood.

The iron slag from the site is of the usual Roman type containing a large proportion of unreduced iron ore. Some pieces were found that showed magnetic properties due to the presence of cast iron produced by allowing too high a temperature to occur in the furnace. Numerous 'core' pieces occurred in which there is a central hole through a length of slag giving a pipe-like effect. These pieces arose from the use of wooden rods to probe or stir up the mass of molten slag in the furnace. When withdrawn these remain as a casing of slag around the burnt-out wood core. A similar phenomenon would probably occur at the holes into the furnace for the nozzles of the crude bellows used to produce the draught, and several large diameter 'cores' found may represent 'core formation' at such points. Several pieces of red clay, partially baked, furnace walls were recovered with pieces of slag still adhering to them.

The pottery found points to an occupation from at least the second century to the end of the Roman period. Besides the common black, grey and terracotta jars, dishes, pots and jugs, there was Samian ware of the Antonine period, showing fish and dolphin motives, Caistor ware, colour-coated ware with white barbotine or slip decoration. Mortaria both in white Salopian and red pseudo-Samian ware occurred. Wine flagons and distinctive wheel-stamped buff ware were found. The occurrence of iron nails, some very large, shoe nails, glass fragments and much charcoal, as well as a Bronze Age thumb scraper, must also be recorded. (Information from C. Scott-Garrett, D. Sc.s.)

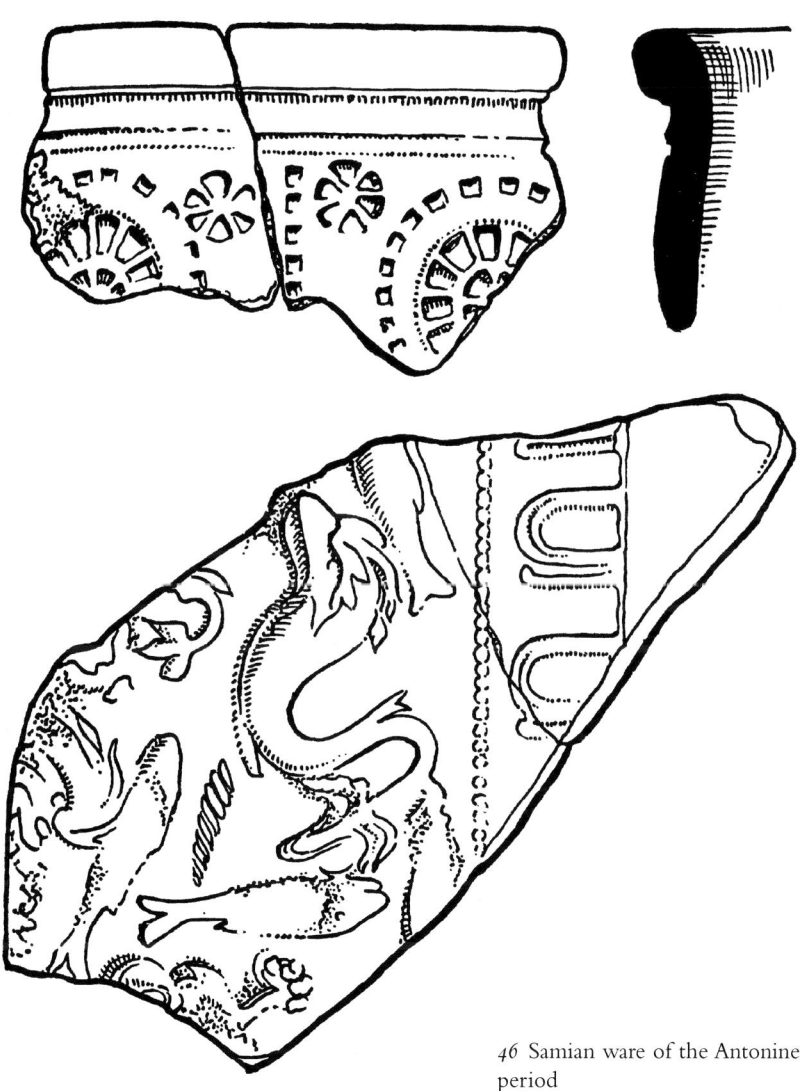

*46* Samian ware of the Antonine period

# APPENDIX 2

# DOWN A CINDER MINE

The Roman and medieval iron industries of Monmouth produced prodigious amounts of waste – bloomery iron slag – which piled up around the town on empty land and especially on the banks of the rivers Monnow and Wye where it also formed islands. One great drift of iron slag is commemorated in Monmouth by 'Cinderhill' Street at Overmonnow.

Bloomery smelting was an inefficient method of making iron (from the Forest of Dean ore) and the resulting slag was consequently rich in the mineral. With the introduction of blast furnaces in the seventeenth century the residual iron could be extracted and one writer at the time estimated that there was sufficient slag lying around, above and below ground, in Monmouth to keep the furnaces supplied for centuries. The slag was sold to forges in the Wye Valley – the cradle of the industrial revolution – including that at Tintern, the remains of which were only recently destroyed during a flood scheme and its millpond filled to make a car park for the Royal George Hotel.

Cinderhill Street today is a perfectly level road but was, at the close of the Middle Ages, made impassable by the 'hill' of iron slag which caused the road to Trelech to detour via what is now Goldwire Lane. The road was further diverted on the south in the eighteenth century when the Council cooperated with the Duke of Beaufort in order to recycle the hill.

Excavations for the New Monnow Bridge in 2003/04 (Clarke and Bray 2004a) revealed just how thoroughly the Cinderhill had been removed. Hardly any iron slag remained along the site of the abutments of the new bridge where 1.20m (4ft) of fine, black dust and charcoal had been left from the riddling of the waste. The slag 'miners' had followed the slag into Roman or medieval features which had been cut into the natural subsoil, totally removing the resource and with it much of the archaeological record. A similar, 1.0m (3ft 3in) thick layer of dust and charcoal was found at The Barton, Trelech (Clarke and Bray 2004b), where the main medieval iron industry was situated.

Excavations were carried out along Granville Street by Monmouth Archaeological Society in the 1960s, prior to the destruction of the Wyeside for the new A449 dual carriageway. The digging revealed several metres of bloomery furnace waste together with the first sealed evidence of Roman smelting in the town – a channel drain from a furnace with an *in situ* slag run.

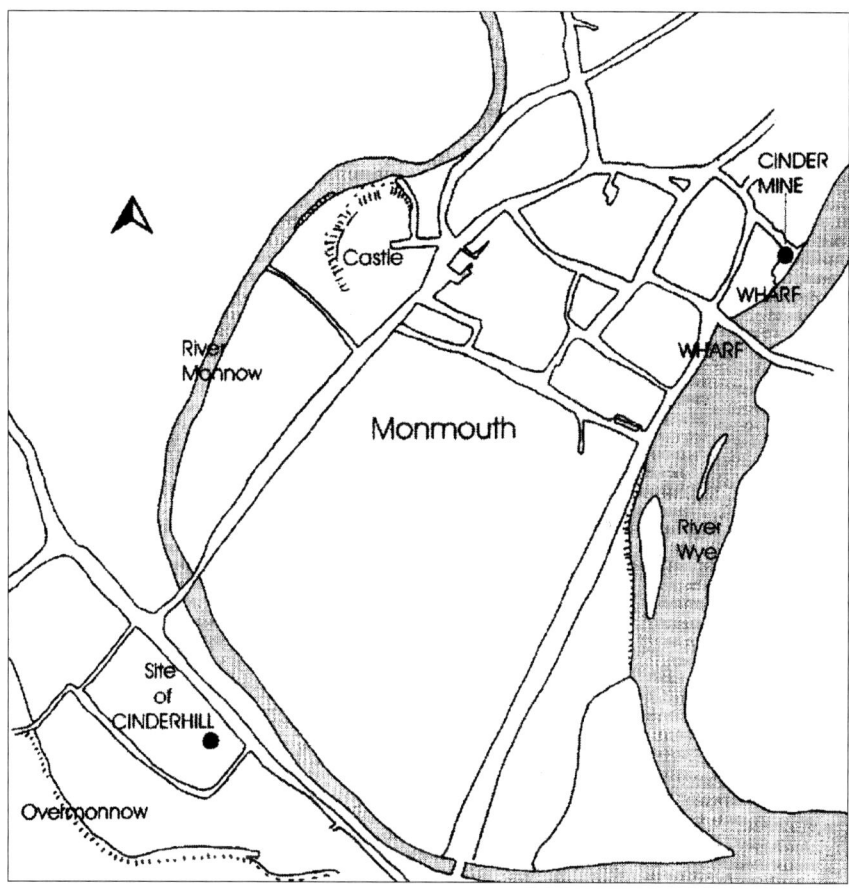

*17* Location plan

During the winter of 2003/04 deep excavations for a sewage chamber and pipeline were carried out on the Quayside near Wye Bridge by AMEC Group Ltd. The excavations encountered over 4m (around 14ft) of undisturbed iron slag without reaching natural ground (Clarke and Bray 2004c). The trench for the pipeline was cut through the foundations of the last warehouse left standing before the Wyeside was destroyed; the works chamber being sited directly over an adjoining bargeman's cottage. The layers of compacted slag underlying the warehouse sloped downwards towards the river, displaying well-defined tip lines and producing occasional sherds of Roman and medieval pottery.

When the excavations reached the site of the cottage it was found that the waste tip lines were dropping back the other way and seventeenth- and eighteenth-century pottery became common. The safety of a pile-driven box allowed the sampling of the various layers which confirmed that the incline of the deposits had been reversed. It was possible to carry out hand digging towards the bottom of the excavation at nearly 4m (around 13ft) below ground level. Here, at the bottom of the slope, the iron slag was solid and almost immovable, even with a pick-axe but above that level a loose layer with black dust and charcoal produced late seventeenth- and early eighteenth-century pottery, bones and 'black jack' wine bottles.

There must have been a 'cinder mine' – the first to be recognised in the field in Monmouth, although they are well recorded in the town archives. For instance in 1769 the Cock Alehouse in this area was offered for sale with its 'iron cinder mine'. The excavations are sometimes referred to as 'cinder pits' and must have been rather like small open-cast coal mines. The sites appear to have been pretty

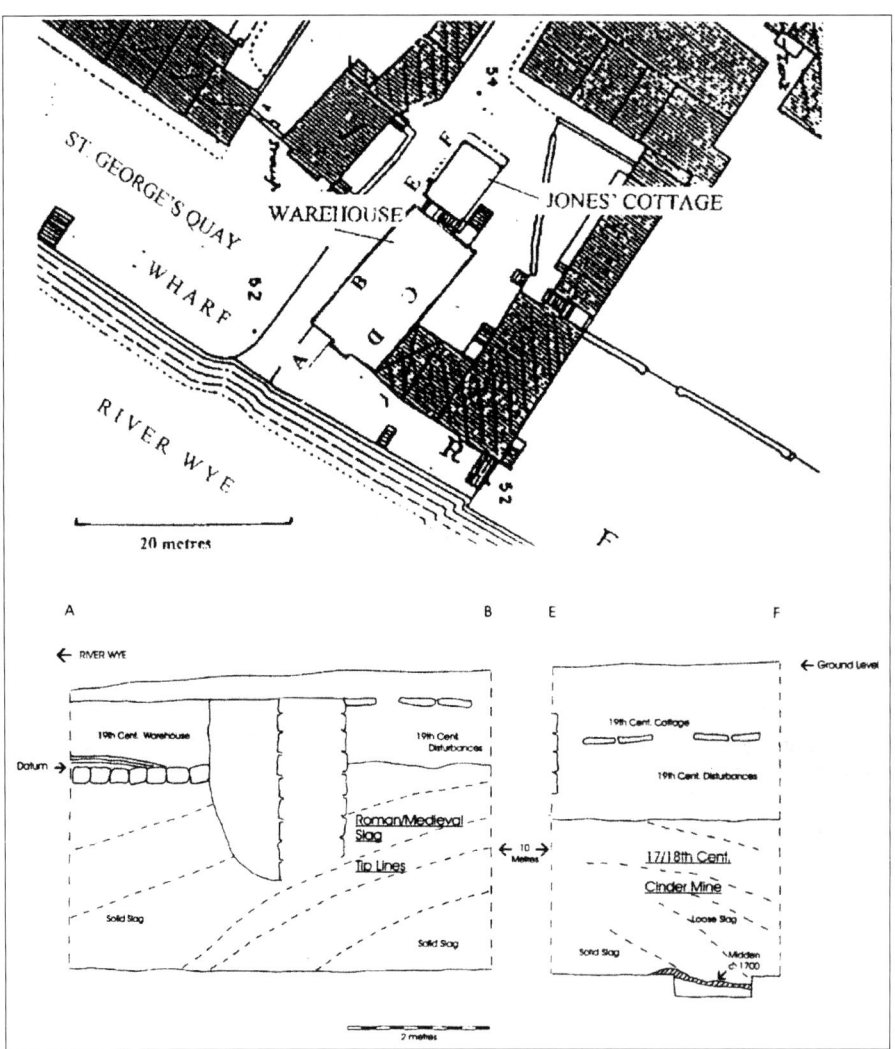

*48* Site plan and sections AB – EF

dangerous after dark as the Council, which was not renowned for its generosity or Health and Safety concerns, paid 1s 6d for the fencing of their mine in 1748!

The abandoned mine would have made an ideal rubbish dump, so its fill could include material of any date but especially that of the declining years of the slag recycling fever.

The pottery from the mine includes the base of a Westerwold stoneware jug or bottle of late seventeenth-/early eighteenth-century date; there are sherds of a Staffordshire moulded slipware plate which in Gloucester has been dated to 1680-90 (Heighway 1983) but at its earliest in Bristol to the 1650s (Barton 1964); there is late seventeenth-/eighteenth-century North Devon gravel tempered ware and a sherd of Newent slipware plate which is also dated to the late seventeenth or the first half of the eighteenth century (Vince 1977). As with the pottery, the glass date range is also late seventeenth/eighteenth century. (Information from Stephen Clark & Jane Bray of Monmouth Archaeology.)

*49* Excavating the cinder mine

*50* Late
seventeenth-/
early eighteenth-
century pottery

*51* The New Monnow Bridge: Roman or medieval feature re-excavated by cinder miners

# APPENDIX 3

# INDUSTRIAL SITES IN THE VALE OF CASTIARD

N.B. The area is now known as the Flaxley Valley.

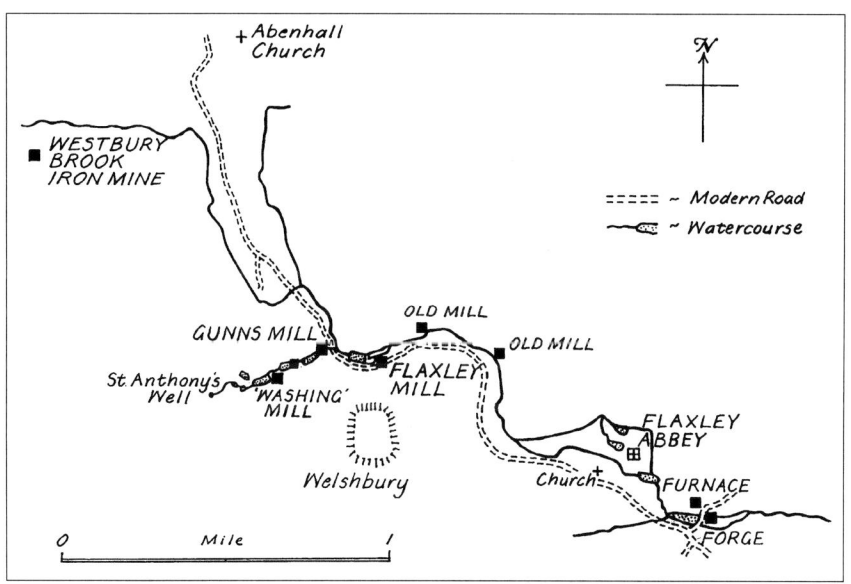

52 Location plan

After leaving Mitcheldean on the road to Flaxley you come to Abenhall church which lies off the road to the left. The church is medieval and the font is a mid-fifteenth-century octagonal bowl with incised shields below with free miners' and smiths' emblems and the noble arms of Buckingham, Warwick and Serjeaunt. On the west wall of the tower is a shield carved with the arms of the free miners which

*53* Abenhall church

*54* Gunns Mill

has recently been renewed. It has been suggested that the presence of the emblems of skilled craftsmen, who always aided in the conduct of wars, may represent an acknowledgment of their faith in the protection of the Church.

As we pass along this valley it is strange to think that, a couple of hundred years ago, the area was highly industrial and, although its aspect has been completely altered for the better, traces of industry can still be found by an informed and observant eye.

The watercourse which flows from near Westbury Iron Mine is joined by another from a spring south of Abenhall church and finally by the one from St Anthony's Well from where the Westbury Brook flows on towards Flaxley. St Anthony's Well was renowned for hundreds of years for its medicinal properties in curing disorders of the skin. It has been said that the monks from Flaxley Abbey also embellished the curative powers of the water in order to gain income for the Abbey. Some of their 'cures' required attendance at the well for several days! The

55 Flaxley Abbey

waters provided power for mills on the by-road, which were a cloth or fulling mill, a paper mill and a possible grist mill. At the junction of the by-road with the Mitcheldean–Flaxley road we come to the more celebrated Gunns Mill, now enveloped in a plastic cover pending restoration work.

Gunns Mill was built by Sir John Winter in 1628-9 and he still held it in 1634. During the Civil War it was run by Captain John Braine in 1644 and was probably destroyed by order of the Commonwealth in 1650. It was certainly a ruin in 1680 and not rebuilt until 1682-3. In the walls of the furnace there are five cast (pig iron) lintels bearing the dates 1682, 1683 and one, which is a little difficult to read, seemingly 1684. Gunns Mill is the best remaining furnace of the earliest period of British blast furnace practice and iron was still cast several times between 1700 and 1732 but, in 1743, the mill was adapted for paper making and steam power was added later.

Flaxley Mill was a grist mill and appears to have been the oldest mill in the valley as it was working in 1207. It is possible that it antedates the function of the Abbey of St Mary de Dene at Flaxley. It is built of local red sandstone, possibly quarried a few hundred yards away at the foot of Shapridge hill. Until 1910 it was still working with an overshot waterwheel.

Iron waste, still containing charcoal, has been found where some furnaces and forges once existed but signs are extremely difficult to identify without detailed knowledge of the surroundings. There were five forges on the brook, two presumably worked by Winter and the others were the property of the owners of the Abbey.

It is said that Matilda, daughter of Henry I, struggled with Stephen for the throne. In this she was helped by Milo, Earl of Hereford, who was given the whole area of Flaxley complete with timber and game as a reward. When Stephen gained the upper hand he did not accept an arrangement made by Matilda so the Royal Hunting Grounds in Gloucestershire returned to the Crown. On Christmas Eve, 1143, Milo was killed by an arrow glancing off a tree in the Flaxley Valley, and his son Roger built Flaxley Abbey in the middle of the twelfth century as a memorial to his father. This was a Cistercian House and probably exercised a great deal of local influence after the monks arrived in the valley in 1154. They certainly became heavily involved in the iron industry. (Information from *Forest of Dean* by F. W. Batty.)

There was a furnace situated just below the Abbey in what was called 'The Furnace Yard' adjoining the park. Some excavation revealed foundation remains and waste from the furnace which ceased operation in 1812.

After the dissolution in 1536 work was carried on by Sir William Kingston in whose family it remained until 1648 when the estate and the iron works were sold to James and William Boevey. It remained in the Boevey family until 1726 when, on the death of Mrs Catherine Boevey, it passed to a cousin, Thomas Crawley, who took the surname of Crawley-Boevey. The estate remained in the Crawley-Boevey family until 1960 when it was purchased by Mr F. B. Watkins. Almost nothing remains of the original Abbey and the appearance today is of subsequent rebuilding.

The road from Flaxley to Blaisdon bears left over a bridge and the dam which retained a very large pool. Waldron Cottage Farm lies on the right-hand bend towards Blaisdon and this is the site of the large Flaxley Iron Forge. Before the farm there was another forge built against the dam wall on the right-hand side of the road, somewhere near where a stone building stands now. A difficult view of one arch through the bridge can be obtained from the south-east side but uncontrolled young tree growth makes it impossible to see anything clearly.

56 Bridge over the Westbury Brook on site of an earlier dam

57 Earlier industrial area of Flaxley

# APPENDIX 4

# INDUSTRIAL SITES ON THE WYE AND MONNOW

The identification of some water-powered iron-producing industrial sites on tributaries of the River Wye and one off the River Monnow is discussed here. The advent of the blast furnace in the early sixteenth century, which required prolonged operation, brought about the construction of water-powered plants. They could not be constructed on the navigable river because the introduction of a weir, to provide a head of water for a mill, would have been expensive and would have interfered with navigation. If a weir was built on the river a lock would also be necessary.

The information contained in this list of industrial sites has been obtained from information researched and prepared by S.D. Coates and D.G. Tucker which was published by the Monmouth Museum Service and is now in their possession. The brief descriptions involved are published by permission of the Curator of Monmouth Museum.

Sites may be followed from the numbers on the Location Plan.

## 1 *Lower or Abbey Forge, SO 529002*
The pond which supplied this site has now been filled in to provide a car park for the hotel and the dam carries the A466 road between Chepstow and Monmouth. Abbey Mill is on the site of Lower or Abbey Forge and had a waterwheel on each side.

## 2 *Lower Abbey Wire Works, SO 526001*
The building, probably part of the wire works, has been demolished. A wall supporting the adjacent road on the southern boundary has several arches and other features which suggest a wheel pit and leat. This was probably the first works to be developed and, when it was completed in July 1567, the building was 50ft (15.24m) long and 30ft (9.14m) wide and had four waterwheels, four hammers and two annealing furnaces. A long leat left the main stream of the Angidy about 546yds (500m) upstream where the remains of the weir can still be seen.

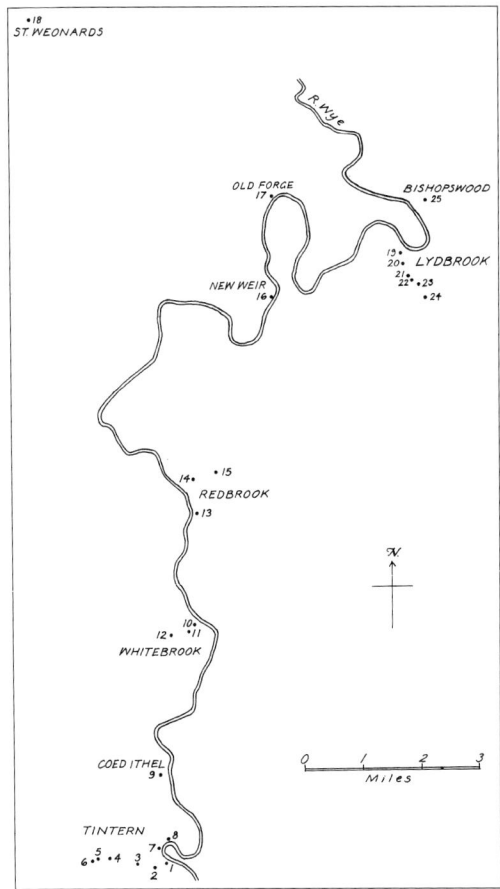

• 18
ST. WEONARDS

R Wye

OLD FORGE
17 •                    BISHOPSWOOD
                        • 25

                    19 •
                    20 •   LYDBROOK
                    21 •
NEW WEIR        22 • • 23
16 •              • 24

              14 •    • 15
                  REDBROOK
                  • 13

                          *N.*

          10 •
12 •    • 11
WHITEBROOK

                    0    1    2    3
COED ITHEL          Miles
9 •

TINTERN        7 • • 8
    5          3 •   1
6 •  • 4        • 2

58 *Left:* Location plan

59 *Below:* Abbey Forge, sketch by
Joseph Powell *c.*1810. *By permission
of Monmouth Museum*

*60* Tintern Abbey
Furnace. Conjectural
drawing by J. Pickin.
*By permission of*
*Monmouth Museum*

### 3 Middle & Chapel Wire Mills, SO 521002

This group of works was served by a wide leat over half a mile long (1km) which can easily be traced from its source. Two mounds of rubble about 40ft (12 m) above the river to the south area are a part of the remains of Middle Wire Mills.

### 4 Blast Furnace, SO 513003

The pond which powered the blast furnace is about 546yds (500m) upstream of the site. Gwent County Council sponsored an excavation of the site in 1979-81 and the uncovered remains revealed the layout of the various buildings. The furnace was in use up until about 1826. At the end of the eighteenth century the bellows were replaced by blowing cylinders – believed to be the first time they were used in this country. Interpretive panels showed the general arrangement of the site.

### 5 Upper Wire Works (or New Tongs Mill), SO 509003

The Upper Wire Works was built about 1803 high on the valley side to the east of the Pont-y-Saeson Works and requiring heavy retaining walls and a very long leat which is easily traced. The main outline of buildings may be seen by the remains of several walls.

### 6 Pont-y-Saeson Forge, SO 508003

There were a number of buildings comprising the works which lay immediately below the dam of the pond which supplied it with water. The dam survives but the pond has been drained and the buildings have almost completely disappeared except for the remnants of some walls.

### 7 Works (probable), SO 528006

There are several illustrations of a mill with a very large waterwheel at Tintern which include a view of the River Wye. The illustration of around 1800 seems to show the mill at the side of the road through the village and, as there are several streams discharging off the hill, the sketch is feasible.

### 8 Works (probable) at Tintern Parva, SO 530008

This is on the Cat Brook where a square stone-built chimney, which seems to have been part of a furnace or kiln, stands among the footings of derelict buildings. Remnants of a pond survive but there is no documentary evidence available.

### 9 Coed Ithel Furnace, SO 528026

About half the shaft of the furnace has survived supported by heavy retaining walls. This may be seen at the roadside some 32ft (10m) above the bed of the stream which powered the blowing machinery. The furnace was at work around 1650 but is thought to have worked for only about 10 years.

### 10 Mill, SO 537067

The purpose of the building is not clear but from the arrangement of the watercourse and the pond it is certain that water power was used. It is possible that this was one of the earlier wirework sites.

*61* Tintern's very large waterwheel. Sketch by Joseph Powell *c.*1810. *By permission of Monmouth Museum*

### 11 Probable Wire Works, SO 536065

A scatter of slag and the remains of several low walls indicate this site was involved in wire production and was likely supplied by a leat from a pond on the Manor Brook.

### 12 Probable Wire Works, SO 531064

A level on the hillside with a number of fragments of stone walls identifies this site which was supplied with water by a long leat which left the Whitebrook just below Sunnyside Mill. The leat roughly follows the 500ft contour, much of which is now a footpath, so that it can be traced in an easterly direction.

### 13 Redbrook Tinplate Works, SO 538097

This large works survived until 1961 when production of the extremely thin handmade tinplate, which had become its speciality, ceased and the works closed. Subsequently the buildings were used for a variety of purposes and slowly deteriorated or were demolished. A plan of Redbrook appears in Appendix 7.

### 14 Furnace Mill, SO 537106

There was a blast furnace in operation here for about 200 years until the early nineteenth century and in 1824 there was a forge and a stamping mill on the site. The stamping mill would have crushed the slag from the blast furnace which was in demand for glass making. Later a foundry and a corn mill operated into the twentieth century.

*62* Redbrook Tinplate Works when the Wye was navigable. *By permission of Monmouth Museum*

## 15  Upper Furnace, SO 544108

The precise location of this furnace is uncertain and it was out of use over 350 years ago. An embankment for the Monmouth Tramroad was subsequently built across the site but some clearance south of the embankment revealed fragments of walling, a possible watercourse and some slag which seems to confirm the possibility of the furnace in that area.

## 16  New Weir Forge, parish of Whitchurch, SO 559156

Undoubted site of ironworking facilities but only fragmentary remains are left. A mill and forge are shown on early maps. It appears to have been built around 1684 by George White, lessee of Monmouth Forge and Thomas Fletcher, both of Monmouth, for the fining of pig iron.

## 17  Old Forge, Whitchurch, SO 559184

This forge was situated on the Garren Brook at confluence with the River Wye. No traces of forge buildings remain but there is cinder and slag in the angle between the Garren and the Wye.

## 18  Old Furnace, St Weonards, SO 494228

A group of farm buildings preclude identification of the precise site but there is a plaque on the buildings, the leat can be identified and there is furnace slag in the area. See Chapter 7 for detail of performance.

## 19  Lower or Lydbrook Forge, SO 5954 1681

This was built about 1610 and an estimate for repairs of 11 June 1760 shows that it was then a chafery, or at least included a chafery. By about 1834 a steam engine had been installed. The nearby Forge Hammer Inn perpetuates the ironworking tradition but no buildings remain which can be identified with ironworking.

## 20  Iron/Tinplate Works, SO 5961 1652

This site produced the first tinplate manufactured at Lydbrook around 1800 but the site has now been completely redeveloped. It was operated as a single manufacturing unit with the works immediately upstream at approximately SO 597162 and finally ceased operation in 1925.

## 21  Middle Forge/Tinplate Works, SO 597(5) 162(0)

Built about 1590 and by 1702 was known as the Upper Forge, consisting of a finery and chafery. At one time it specialised in making Osmond iron for the wire works at Tintern and Whitebrook, and in about 1625 was producing wire itself. Before starting the manufacture of tinplate in association with the works below it, it was known as the Rolling Mill and possibly also as Lower Forge. By 1834 a steam engine was in use but the lower tinplate works seem to have become the more important unit. By the end of the century the works were closed and eventually demolished.

### 22 Wire works, SO 598161

This was built around 1818–20 as a wire works extension of the iron works a short distance upstream. The works was served by a large pond and produced wire for fencing, and later for telegraph use. As a result of poor trade the works closed in the last decade of the nineteenth century.

### 23 Iron works, SO 600160

The works were purchased from the Crown in 1818 and subsequently improved. Iron for agricultural purposes, smith work and horse nails were produced. By 1880 some 50 men were employed with the main market being Birmingham. Along with the adjacent wire works the business closed in 1890–1900.

### 24 Upper Forge, SO 602156

This was built around 1590 but had a relatively short life and by 1668 had disappeared. By 1702 the name 'Upper Forge' had been transferred to the Middle Forge.

### 25 Bishopswood Furnace, SO 602183

Iron was made here by blast furnace by at least the last decade of the sixteenth century but the precise position of the works is not known. A blast furnace was operating in the latter part of the seventeenth century but it is believed to have ceased usage by 1751. Several travellers reported passing: 'an iron-work called Bishop's Wood Furnace, and observe several pigs of iron ready to be conveyed to the barges'. A branch of the Severn and Wye Railway to the iron works was authorised in 1810 but smelting had apparently ceased by 1814. There was also a forge at Bishopswood from an early date which survived until 1816 at which point its stock of iron was removed by the Severn and Wye Railway Company to defray its debts.

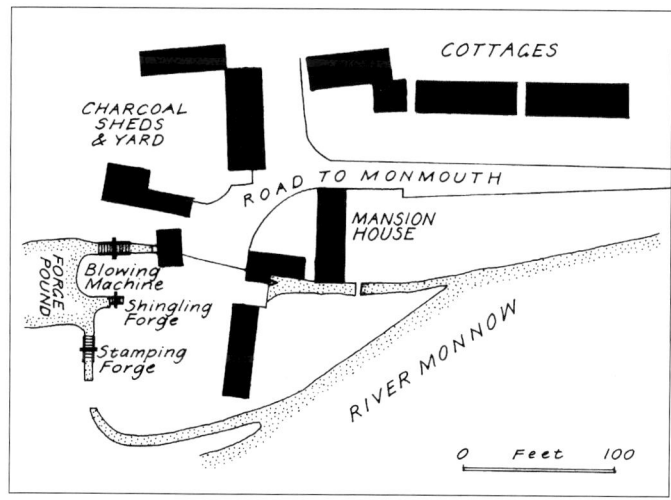

63 Monmouth Forge 1849

# APPENDIX 5

# THE THREE CASTLES

In Chapter 4 we discussed the manufacture of large numbers of quarrels for crossbows in the thirteenth century at St Briavels castle which, in the early warfare and the campaigns against Wales, was the king's armament depot. One of the reasons for the importance of St Briavels manufacturing quarrels was the necessary importance of the Three Castles: Grosmont, Skenfrith and White Castle, and they featured in many military orders that were recorded. The strategic importance of the castles was due to the fact that they lay in an area of the Welsh border that the Normans had identified as somewhat open, as the land was relatively level around the River Monnow, and offered a route via Monmouth to access South Wales. The early history of the castles was disorganised and it was not until the late twelfth century that written records exist of the Three Castles. In the early thirteenth

*64* Grosmont Castle

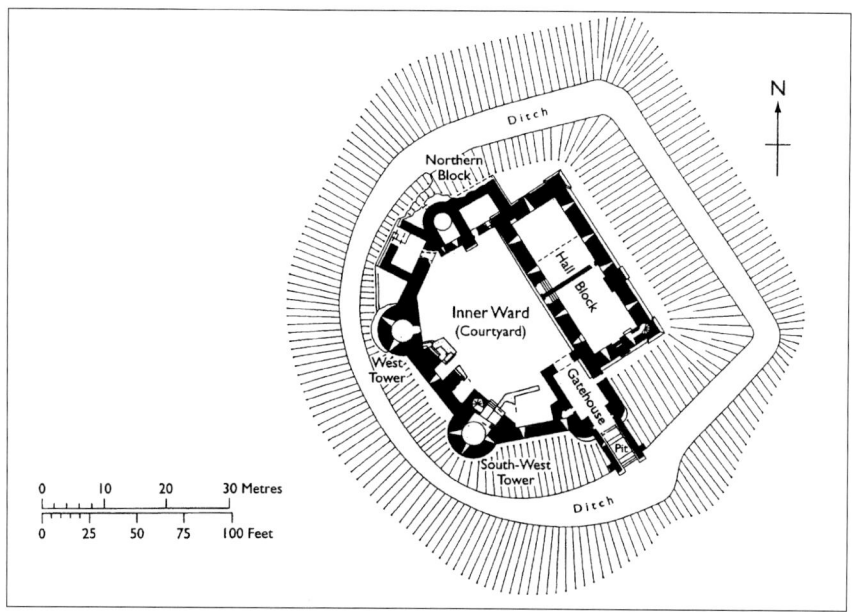

65 Plan of Grosmont Castle. *Cadw (Crown Copyright)*

century Hubert de Burgh, after many experiences elsewhere, was appointed to manage the castles and it was at this point that the early bank and timber defences and inner buildings were replaced by stone ones.

Grosmont Castle stands on a raised hillock, slightly above the village, and is reached by a footpath which climbs up to it. It is likely that the village was a Norman foundation established for their own purposes. The castle contained residential accommodation, presumably for de Burgh's convenience.

The entirety of Skenfrith Castle was built by de Burgh as a previous 'earth and timber' castle appears to have been demolished prior to the stone construction in around 1219/1232. Skenfrith contained domestic accommodation and an upper room in the distinctive round keep appeared to have been for a person of 'high status'. The Monnow River runs alongside the north-east wall.

White Castle is quite enormous compared with its companions and was presumably constructed of stone, following the removal of the 'earth and timber' castle in the thirteenth century. There were some radical changes undertaken at that time with the previous entrance from the south being repositioned on the north side. The outer Ward was originally more extensive than the present one and it seems likely that the castle was principally an army base as there are records showing many quarrels being delivered and stored there.

66 Skenfrith Castle

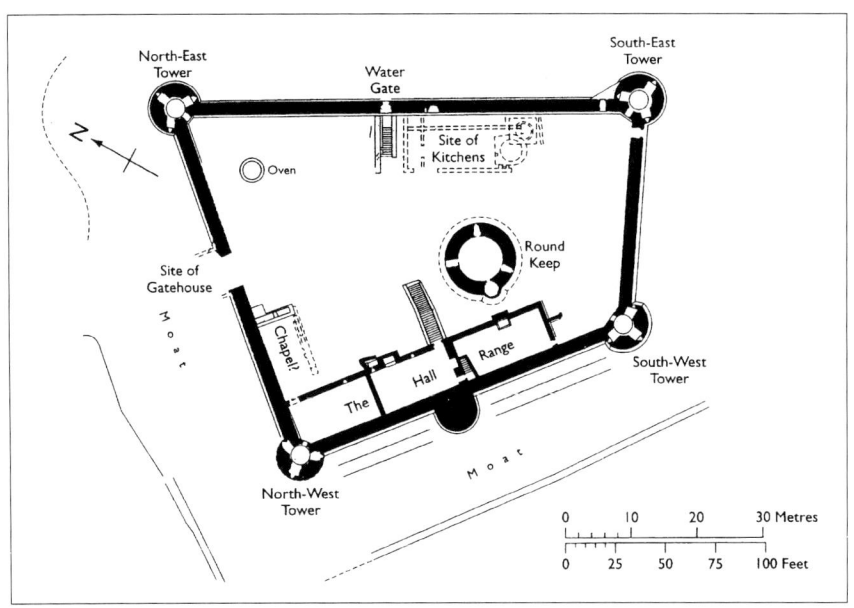

67 Plan of Skenfrith Castle. *Cadw (Crown Copyright)*

*Opposite*
68 The Inner Ward of White Castle
69 Plan of White Castle. *Cadw (Crown Copyright)*

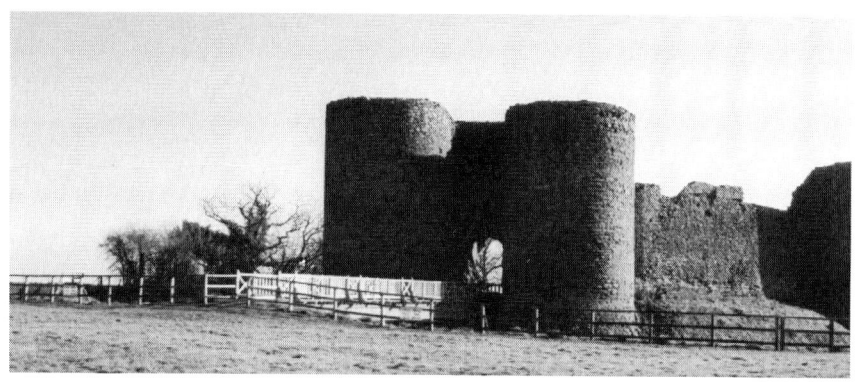

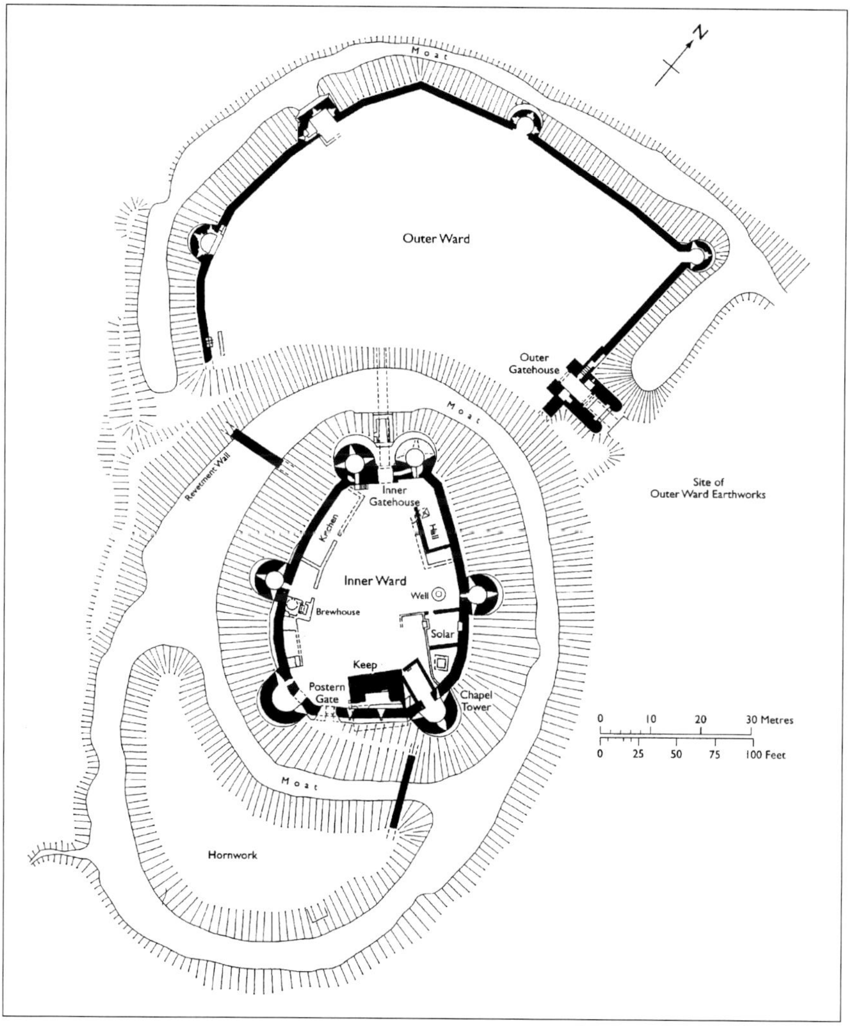
N
Moat
Outer Ward
Outer Gatehouse
Moat
Site of Outer Ward Earthworks
Revetment Wall
Inner Gatehouse
Kitchen
Hall
Inner Ward
Well
Brewhouse
Solar
Keep
Postern Gate
Chapel Tower
0 10 20 30 Metres
0 25 50 75 100 Feet
Moat
Hornwork

# APPENDIX 6

# LOCAL HERITAGE SOURCES

After encountering the diversity of information on the iron industry, and developing the story of the industry in the first part of this book, it is encouraging to find evidence of heritage emerging which is open to all. The Dean Heritage Centre contains a wealth of material on all aspects of Dean history and has an interesting display on iron production and charcoal burning. The buildings are on a site known as Camp Mill, the name being derived from the Norman camp nearby. There is a history, from around the early seventeenth century, of the site being involved in the iron industry and subsequently as a flour mill, a leatherboard factory and sawmill. The building shown in figure 70 was the leatherboard factory.

There are interesting open days at the Dean Heritage Centre when iron is produced by the bloomery method, and charcoal is produced and later bagged and sold!

70 Dean Heritage Centre

*71* Pavement mosaic – the industrial past

A visitor to Coleford will find several very interesting and informative walks scheduled by the Coleford Tourist Information Centre, some of which cover the memory of David and Robert Mushet who were discussed previously. The earliest settlers to the site of Coleford would have found abundant water – it is the confluence of three streams which have since been culverted – and abundant iron ore and timber. The name was Colevorde in 1275 and it was not included in *Domesday Book* in 1086, as it was then part of the king's forest. Starting from the clock tower in the centre of Coleford you may pass through a wrought iron screen bearing the caption 'Mushets Walk'. The path travels between buildings and contains mosaics which display features of industrial history. One shows towers and railway lines and celebrates the Forest's industrial past. Another, with a strong chain and industrial wheels commemorates the mining industries of the area which obviously includes iron. This walk was created through a Coleford Town Council project and the mosaics were designed by students at the Royal Forest of Dean College.

A walk up Cinder Hill, beyond the Mushet's house, now the Forest House Hotel, takes you to Mushet Place on your right. Here there is a plaque commemorating the work of Robert Forester Mushet in a barn on that site where he perfected the Bessemer Process of steel manufacture and discovered self-hardening steel.

Parkend Iron Works had an illustrious life, and its beginnings were mentioned in Chapter 6. David Mushet had complimented the quality of hot-blast iron in 1874

72  Pavement mosaic – the mining industries

73  Robert Forester Mushet plaque

*74* Parkend engine house

and Edwin Crawshay purchased the plant in 1875, but events turned against it and the depression forced its closure in August 1877. The furnaces were demolished in 1890 and the last stack pulled down in 1908. In the same year the engine house – seen in figure 76 covered in red creeper – was converted to a Forester Training School and later, into a field studies centre.

The deposit of iron ore is part of the geological history of Dean and a full explanation of all the many rock formations, all affected by powerful earth movements, in the Soudley Valley is available from the Gloucestershire Geoconservation Trust. They produce a geological pamphlet on the valley where the walk they direct will take one through almost 100 million years of the Earth's history! Crease Limestone is also visible on the walk, from which iron ore was extracted, and the inundation of the sea to cover the land and the sequences of uplift and subsidence are also explained.

Finally a visit to Clearwell Caves, the Royal Forest of Dean's Iron Mining Museum, allows a visitor to gain first-hand experience of conditions which surrounded the extraction of ochre and iron ore. The entrance marks a point at which early miners followed the iron ore underground, once the surface ore had been exhausted, by following the irregular course of the ore through the Crease Limestone.

The Museum produces an explanatory pamphlet which gives details of all the colourful aspects of the 'churns' through which you will pass. Ochre was said to be the principal product of the mine with ore as a secondary product. Some ore for experimental purposes and educational samples is still produced along with ochre for artist's paints.

There are provisions for caving trips to the deeper levels of Clearwell Caves. These are led by experienced guides and, while being strenuous, the variety of

75 Entrance to Clearwell Caves

*76* An underground 'churn' in Clearwell Caves

interest in the caves makes this an exciting experience. At the exit from the mine the Mine Shop has a good range of appropriate minerals and information on local history. It is worth remembering that this mine could have been in use from the Neolithic period which began around 4500 BC.

*77* The new monument to the iron miners, coal miners and stone quarrymen of the Forest of Dean

# APPENDIX 7

# HISTORICAL ACCOUNTS

N.B. The following two accounts are taken from *Iron Making in the Forest of Dean*, Nicholls 1867.

*Historical Account 1*
In 1683 Sir John Erule, the Forest supervisor, renewed the Commissioner's original proposal that the Crown should become involved in ironmaking in Dean, but it was rejected. In fact the authorities were so determined to save the Forest timber that they directed the demolition of the Forest furnaces to such an extent that it would have annihilated them for at least a hundred years. Andrew Yarranton, in his book *Improvements of England by Sea and Land* which had been printed in 1677, had recorded the state of prosperity which then existed. He stated:

> And first, I will begin in Monmouthshire, and go through the Forest of Dean, and there take notice what infinite quantities of raw iron is there made, with bar iron and wire; and consider the infinite number of men, horses and carriages which are to supply these works, and also digging of ironstone, providing of cinders, carrying to the works, making it into sows and bars, cutting of wood and converting into charcoal. Consider also, in all these parts, the woods are not worth the cutting and bringing home by the owner to burn in their houses; and it is because in all these places there are pit coal very cheap. If these advantages were not there, it would be little less than a howling wilderness. I believe if this comes to the hands of Sir Baynom Frogmorton [Throgmorton] and Sir Duncomb Colchester, they will be on my side. Moreover, there is yet a most great benefit to the kingdom in general by the sow iron made of the ironstone and Roman cinders in the Forest of Dean, for that metal is of a most gentle, pliable, soft nature, easily and quickly to be wrought into manufacture, over what any other iron is, and it is the best in the known world; and the greatest part of this sow iron is sent up Severne to the forges into Worcester, Shropshire, Staffordshire, Warwickshire and Cheshire, and there it's made into bar iron; and because of its kind and gentle nature to work, it is now at Sturbridge, Dudley, Wolverhampton, Sedgley, Wasall and Burmingham, and there bent, wrought and manufactured into all small commodities, and diffused all England over, and thereby a great trade made of it; and, when manufactured, into most parts of the world. And I can very easily make

it appear, that in the Forest of Dean and thereabouts, and about the material that comes from thence, there are employed and have their subsistence therefrom no less than 60,000 persons. And certainly, if this be true, then it is certain it is better these iron works were up and being than that there were none. And it were well if there were an Act of Parliament for enclosing all common fir, or any likely to bear wood in the Forest of Dean and six miles round the Forest; and that great quantities of timber might by the same law be there preserved, for to supply in future ages timber for shipping and building. And I dare say the Forest of Dean is, as to the iron, to be compared to the sheep's back as to the woollen; nothing being of more advantage to England than these two are .... In the Forest of Dean and thereabouts, the iron is made this day of cinders, being the rough and offal thrown by in the Romans' time; they then having only foot blasts to melt the iron stone; but now, by the force of a great wheel that drives a pair of bellows 20ft long, all that iron is extracted out of the cinders, which could not be forced from it by the Roman foot blast. And in the Forest of Dean and thereabouts, and as high as Worcester, there are great and infinite quantities of these cinders, some in vast mounts above ground, some underground, which will supply the iron works some hundreds of years, and these cinders are they which make the prime and best iron, and with much less charcoal than doth the ironstone.

## Historical Account 2

With respect to the manner then in use of reducing the mine ore, a very explicit account remains from the pen of Dr Parsons, the county antiquary and naturalist of that age, published around 1683, and included here with regard to the detail it contains.

The ore and cinder, wherewith they make their iron [which is the great employment of the poorer sort of inhabitants], 'tis dug in most parts of the Forest, one in the bowels, and the other towards the surface of the earth. There are two sorts of ore; the best ore is your Brush ore, of blewish colour, very ponderous, and full of shiny specks like grains of silver; this affordeth the greatest quantity of iron, but being melted alone, produceth a metal very short and brittle. To remedy this inconvenience, they make use of another material, which they call cinder, it being nothing else but the refuse of the ore after the melting hath been extracted, which, being melted with the other in due quantity, gives it that excellent temper of toughness for which this iron is preferred before any other that is brought from foreign parts.

After they have provided their ore, their first work is to calcine it which is done in kilns, much after the fashion of our ordinary lime kilns; these they fill up to the top with coal and ore until it be full, and so, putting fire to the bottom, they let it burn till the coal be wasted, and then renew the kilns with fresh ore and coal. This is done without any infusion of metal, and serves to consume the more drossy part of the ore, and to make it fryable supplying the beating and washing, which are to no other metals; from hence they carry it to their furnaces which are built of brick and stone, about 24ft square on the outside and near 30ft in height within, and not above 8 or 10ft over where it is widest, which is about the middle, the top and bottom having a narrow compass, much like the form of an egg. Behind the furnace are placed two high pair of bellows, whose noses meet at a little hole near the bottom; these are compressed together by certain buttons placed on the axis of a very large wheel, which is turned round by water in the manner of a over-shot mill. As soon as these buttons are slid off the bellows are raised again by a counterpoise of weights, whereby they are made to play alternately, the one giving its blast while the other is rising.

At first they fill these furnaces with ore and cinder intermixt with fuel, which in these works is always charcoal, laying them hollow at the bottom, that they may the more easily take fire; but after they are once kindled the materials run together into an hard cake or lump, which is sustained by the furnace, and through this the metal as it trickles down the receivers, which are placed at the bottom, where there is a passage open, by which they take away the scum and dross, and let out their metal as they see occasion.

Before the mouth of the furnace lyeth a great bed of sand, where they make furrows of the fashion they desire to cast their iron; into these, when the receivers are full, they let in their metal, which is made so very fluid by the violence of the fire that it not only runs to a considerable distance but stands afterwards boiling a great while.

After these furnaces are once at work, they keep them constantly employed for many months together, never suffering the fire to slacken night or day, but still supplying the waste of fuel and other materials with fresh, poured in at the top.

Several attempts have been made to bring in the use of sea coal in these works, instead of charcoal; the former being to be had at an easy rate, the latter not without a great expence, but hitherto they have proved ineffectual, the workmen finding by experience that a sea-coal fire, how vehement soever, will not penetrate the most fixed parts of the ore, by which means they leave much of the metal behind them unmelted.

From these furnaces they bring the sows and piggs of iron, as they call them, to their forges; these are two sorts though they stood together under the same roof; one they call their finery and the other chafers; both of them are upon hearths, upon which they place great heaps of sea coal, and behind them bellows like those of the furnaces, but nothing near so large.

In such finerys they first put their piggs of iron, placing three or four of them together behind the fire, with a little of one end thrust into it, where softening by degrees they stir and work them with long bars of iron till the metal runs together in a round mass or lump, which they call an half bloome; this they take out, and giving it a few strokes with their sledges, they carry it to a great weighty hammer, raised likewise by the motion of a water wheel, where, applying it dexterously to the blows, they presently beat it into a thick short square; this they put into the finery again, and heating it red hot, they work it under the same hammer till it comes to the shape of a bar in the middle with two square knobs in the ends; last of all they give it other heatings in the chaffers, and more working under the hammer, till they have brought their iron into bars of several shapes, in which fashion they expose them to sale.

All their principal iron undergoes the aforementioned preparations, yet for several other purposes, as for backs of chimneys, hearths of ovens, and the like they have a sort of cast iron which they take out of the receivers of the furnace so soon as it is melted, in great ladles and pour it into the moulds of fine sand in the like manner as they do cast brass and softer metals; but this sort of iron is so very brittle, that, being heated with one blow of the hammer, it breaks all to pieces.

# APPENDIX 8

# DISTRICT MAPS

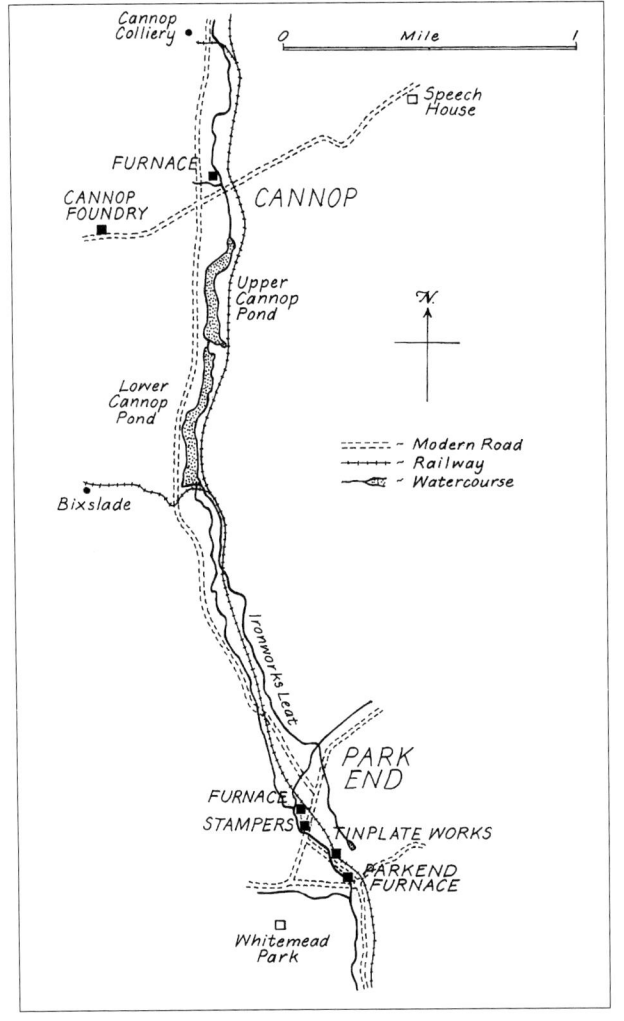

Presented here are a number of district maps covering a wide range of time but presenting a picture of iron industry locations together with other related sites.

78 Cannop and Parkend

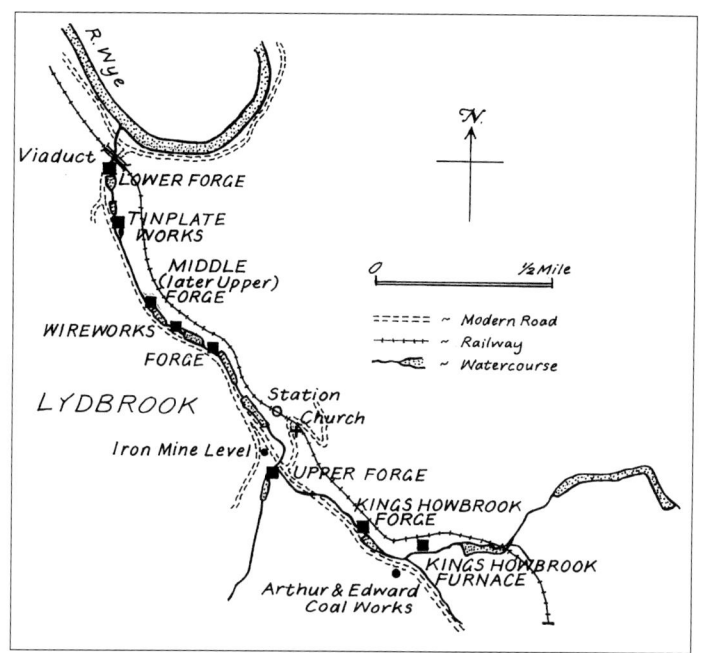

79 Lydbrook

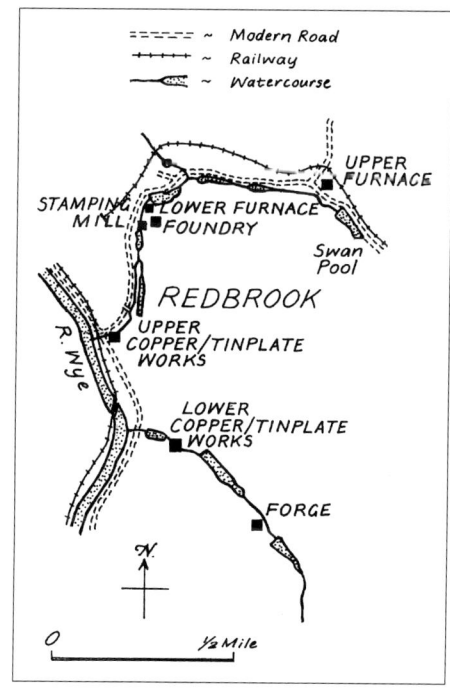

80 Upper and Lower Redbrook

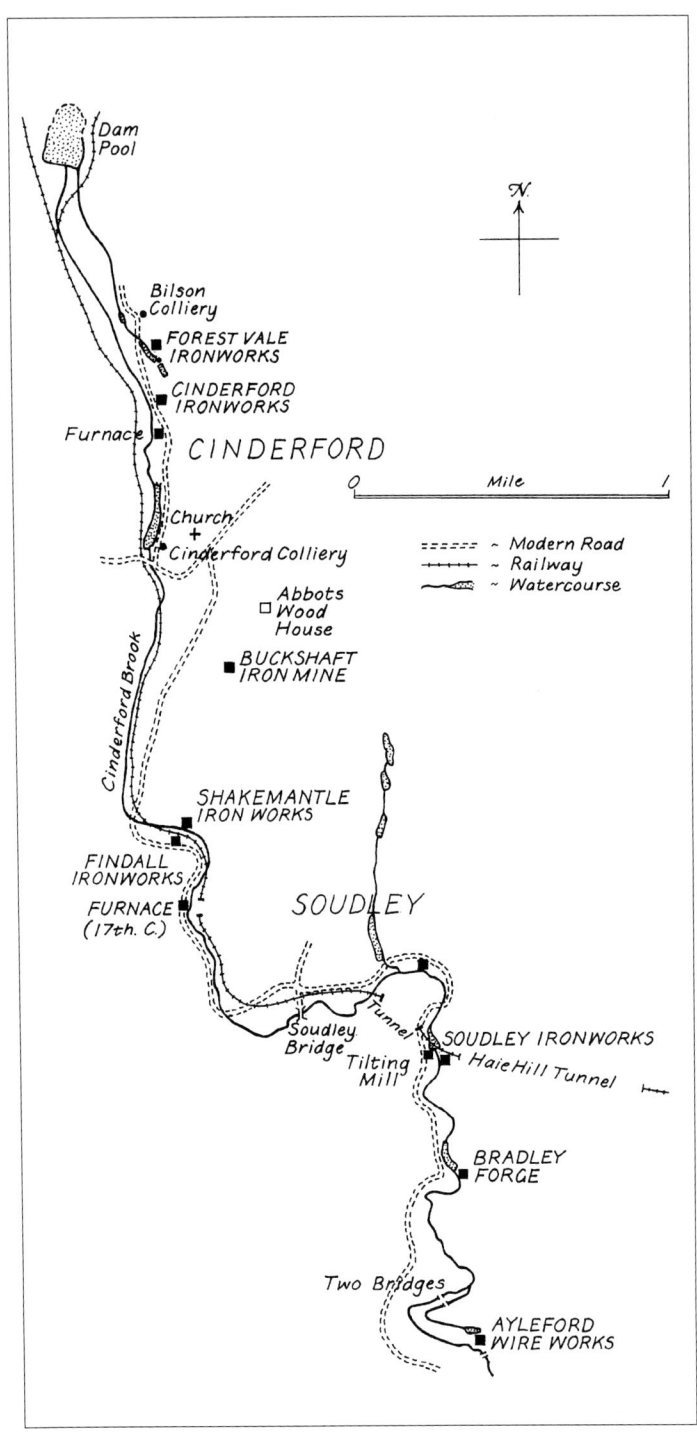

*81* Cinderford,
Soudley and
Ayleford

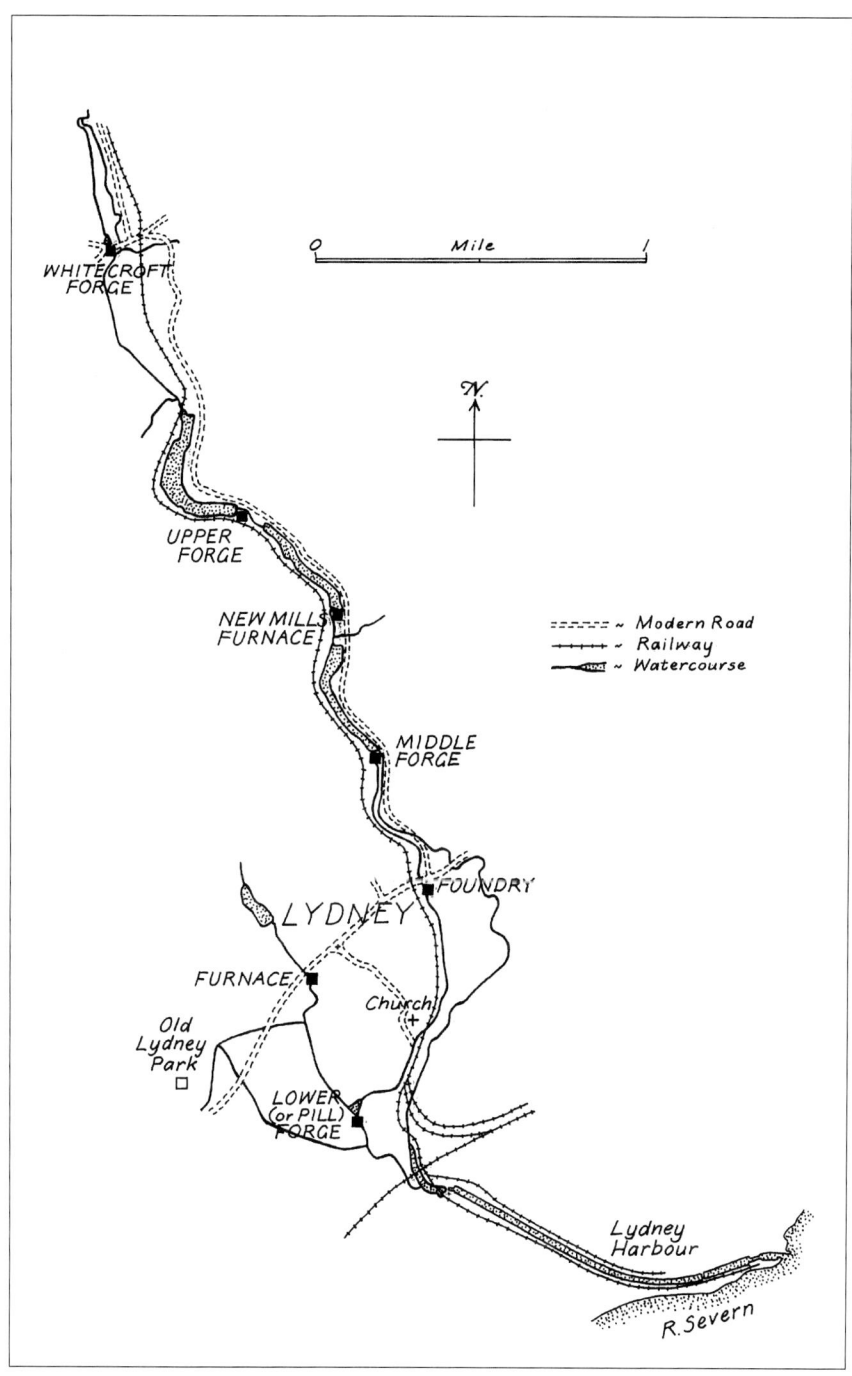

*82* Lydney

# SELECT BIBLIOGRAPHY

Anstis, R. (1997) *Man of Iron – Man of Steel, The lives of David and Robert Mushet*. Pub. Albion House, Coleford, Gloucestershire.

Cunliffe, B. (second edition 1978) *Iron Age Communities in Britain*. Pub. Routledge & Kegan Paul, London.

Cunliffe, B. and Nash, D. (1984) in *Cross Channel Trade Between Gaul and Britain in the Pre-Roman Iron Age*. Pub. The Society of Antiquaries of London.

Hart, C. (1972) *The Industrial History of Dean*. Pub. David & Charles, Newton Abbot.

Knight, J. (1991 and 2000) *The Three Castles*. Pub. CADW, Welsh Historic Monuments.

Nicholls, Rev. H.G. (1867), Facsimile (1981) *Iron Making in the Forest of Dean*. Pub. Douglas McLean, The Forest Bookshop.

Schubert, H.R. (1957) *History of the British Iron and Steel Industry*. Pub. Routledge & Kegan Paul, London.

Walters, B. (1992) *The Forest of Dean Iron Industry, lst to 4th Centuries AD, Parts 1 and 2*. Pub. Dean Archaeological Group Occasional Publication No 4.

Webb, K. (2001) *Robert Mushet and the Darkhill Ironworks*. Black Dwarf Publications, Lydney, Gloucestershire.

# INDEX